Problem So ies 2

Key Stage Two/Primary Three–Six

Contents

Teacher's Notes

Introduction

The implementation of the National Curriculum in England, the Northern Ireland Curriculum and the National Guidelines for 5-14 in Scotland, have placed enormous demands on primary school teachers. One aspect of the mathematics curriculum that tends to create the most difficulty for teachers to interpret and prepare for, is Attainment Target 1, (now Ma 1), 'Using and applying' which relates to problem-solving. Problem-solving is one of the least understood aspects of mathematics, being multi-faceted and ill-defined. Yet it is an activity that should be integrated into all aspects of the learning process. It involves more than the solving of a problem. It is a composite of all the learning processes, combined to achieve the problem's solution – a solution that may not be immediately obvious and for which there is often no readily available formula.

The National Curriculum requires all schools to address the issue of problem-solving and schemes of work must offer sufficient opportunities for developing problem-solving and investigational strategies.

This book has been designed to develop logical thinking strategies in children. It consists of a series of games and puzzles that combine to make a useful addition to any classroom mathematics programme. Games and puzzles are a highly practical and motivational way of developing problem-solving skills.

Aims of problem-solving games.

- the growth of problem-solving strategies;
- a heightened mathematical awareness;
- the development of positive self-concepts;
- a sense of gamesmanship;
- a respect for the feelings and abilities of others;
- an appreciation of the need for rules and procedures for the playing of games;
- the development of personal qualities such as independence, perseverance and an ability to co-operate.

Skills for problem-solving

Problem-solving requires the development of skills to investigate or to solve puzzles, some of which have a definite answer and some of which have a range of possible solutions. It involves an exploratory approach to learning in which the process of solving the problem becomes as important as the solution to the problem. The Non-Statutory Guidance (1989) for Mathematics in the National Curriculum identified three interrelated strands in the development of such skills: 'Using mathematics', 'Communicating in mathematics' and 'Developing ideas of argument and proof'.

In order to develop skills of problem-solving, pupils might be required to:

- identify the problem or interpret instructions;
- talk about the task and ask questions related to the task;
- identify the knowledge they have which might solve the problem;
- predict possible outcomes based on their experience;
- test predictions;
- devise methods of recording results;
- explain their work and give reasons;
- approach the task systematically;
- generalise results.

Stages and strategies of problem-solving

Teachers and pupil problem-solvers may identify three phases in the process of solving a puzzle or pursuing a task:

Initial phase
This phase consists of understanding the problem, deciding what is required to achieve the problem's solution and, possibly, clarifying the problem.

Central phase
This phase consists of tackling the problem by working out a plan, carrying it through and monitoring the outcome. The problem-solver may experience difficulties if the plan is unworkable. The problem-solver needs to realise that a natural part of tackling problems is the discovery that a different route may be required than that originally chosen. There may be a need for 'trial and improvement' methods until a satisfactory solution can be obtained.

Concluding phase
This phase consists of reflecting on the methods used to solve the problem. The problem-solver may use the experience gained to extend the problem or to create opportunities to improve the solution.

Children may be observed working through these phases as they experience the games or activities in this book.

Problem-solving and assessment

Assessment of the skills required in problem-solving activities might be considered to be more difficult than assessment of other aspects of mathematics, as there may be no direct route in arriving at a solution to a problem. Children are often led in different directions, depending on their previous experiences, skills and the way in which they perceive the problem.

Children's written records of the strategies they use in order to reach a successful outcome when playing a game may be assessed by the teacher against the National Curriculum Statements of Attainment. However, a more coherent picture of children's problem-solving skills may be achieved by the inclusion of the teacher's observational assessment. When pupils are engaged in small-group work the teacher has some freedom to circulate about the class. It may be appropriate to focus on a particular group on a given day and to use the *Teacher's checklist* in this book to monitor individual pupil's mathematical processes and disposition.

A pupil's own observations are also a valuable contribution to comprehensive assessment profile. Information gathered from observational assessment, in addition to any written or diagrammatical evidence, can be used to inform teaching or to identify a pupil's needs. The *Pupil's own checklist* may be a useful way of collecting pupil feedback.

As pupils talk about their experiences – as they explain, argue, predict and reason about what they are doing – the teacher has a valuable opportunity to gain insight into the development of attitudes and mathematical thinking.

How to use this book

The games and activities in this book have been chosen for their suitability for children. They offer 'fun' opportunities for pupils to practise and develop strategy techniques for problem-solving. They are easily learned but not easily mastered. Rules are deliberately simple to enable children to refer to them if necessary.

In general, the activities fall into three categories:

Alignment activities – in which players place markers on the gameboard according to specific information requirements.

Configuration activities – in which players make entries on the gameboard according to specific configuration requirements.

Withdrawal activities – in which players delete elements from the gameboard according to stated rules.

Some activities are designed to be completed by pupils on their own and some activities are for pairs of children or small groups.

Teachers should select games or activities for inclusion in their mathematics curriculum on the basis of relevance, purpose and suitability.

Teachers need to understand the game characteristics prior to introducing any activity, as this is an aid in explaining puzzle procedures, dealing with problems as they arise and leading individual, group or class discussions.

The exploring of varied strategies and approaches in solving particular problems is essential if skills are to be generated and called upon in all subject areas.

The 39 photocopiable worksheets in this book consist of instructions for playing 23 problem-solving games, plus gameboards for 15 of the games. Where a game has both instructions and a gameboard, these have been placed on facing pages so that they can be photocopied together onto one A3 sheet, if desired.

Resources required are minimal, and therefore easy to provide: counters, paper, coloured pencils or crayons.

Children can work at their own level as no computational skills are required. All that is needed is an understanding of the object of the game and the procedures for playing the game.

Getting started in the classroom

Having chosen an activity and having experienced how to play the game, the teacher may decide:

- to structure games sessions during which all the children are playing games – they may be playing the same game, or different groups may be playing different games;
- to build a game into a group's programme of work;
- to build a game into a class session where each group is involved in a different mathematical activity;
- to offer opportunities for free-choice of an activity or game.

Introducing the activity

Teachers may decide:

- to demonstrate the playing of a game by using an overhead projector if the activity is for the whole class;
- to demonstrate on a blackboard, whiteboard or flip chart for a class or a number of groups;
- to demonstrate by using a photocopied gameboard and playing the game with a group;
- to encourage a group of children, who have already played a game, to demonstrate and explain the rules to another group;
- to encourage the children to interpret the rules of a new game for themselves. (Children should have experienced playing a number of games prior to this.)

Some thought may be given to how to decide who should make the first move in the game so that members of the group feel it is a 'fair' process. Possible suggestions are:

- throwing a die;
- using a spinner;
- drawing a card from a pack of cards;
- tossing a coin.

Grouping for the activity

Children may be grouped according to a number of criteria but it is helpful to create different grouping arrangements for different games activities throughout the mathematics programme. Teachers may decide to arrange groups by:

- asking one child to choose the other players for his or her group (and ensuring opportunities for different children to do the choosing!);

- selecting groups of friends who co-operate with each other well;
- selecting members of the group on the basis of personality (such as ensuring dominant children play with dominant children or placing shy children in a supportive group, etc);
- selecting children who are of similar mathematical ability to work together.

Communication

Each game should be clearly explained to all players so that everyone is confident about the procedure or rules. (Children who are unsure of what is expected become inhibited at the risk of appearing ignorant.) When children have become confident at playing games and are showing signs of developing strategies to win, they may be encouraged to explain rules to other groups or begin to attempt to interpret the rules of a new game for themselves. These are important aspects of 'Using and applying', interpreting, explaining and reporting. Therefore, it is important that teachers create opportunities for this to occur, and to monitor children's progress. Teachers need to encourage players:

- to wait for their turn patiently;
- to move only their own counter unless required to do otherwise;
- to quietly offer help to another player where appropriate.

Feedback

Talking with the children is the best way to find out the extent of their understanding and any difficulties. Class and/or group discussion may be appropriate. There should be opportunities to share satisfaction and frustration. Children should come to realise that, if they enjoy playing the game, it does not matter if they do not always win. What they should gain is an insight into how to approach a variety of games or activities which require the development of a strategy for a successful outcome. Children thrive in an environment of understanding, encouragement and challenge.

Where appropriate, children could keep a record of their 'moves' on a photocopy of the gameboard worksheet.

Extension

Prompts which teachers might consider to develop children's mathematical thinking would include:

- devising appropriate ways to record how a puzzle was solved;
- discussing winning strategies;
- counting the number of moves needed to win a game;
- finding the least number of moves required for a desired outcome;
- extending the puzzle or investigation.

Further suggestions

Teachers may consider creating an activity area in the classroom where these problem-solving activities are available, as a way of stimulating and interesting children.

Games and puzzles may be available for children who have completed work and have some time to spare before introduction to another activity. Little supervision is required as the games demand concentrated effort on the part of the pupils.

The activities in this book could be a focus on special mathematics 'fun days' for a year group or a whole school.

As the resources for each activity are easily provided, children could be encouraged to take them home and share their experiences with a friend or member of the family. This would be a superb opportunity for children to demonstrate the development of their mathematical thinking.

1

POLYCHROME

Aim

To be the last player able to colour an area so that it is not next to an area of the same colour.

Number of players

2

Materials

Paper, two, three or four coloured pencils.

Play

Starter: first player draws the playing area and divides it into an arbitrary number of segments (15 – 20) (see 'Gameboard').
– second player decides how many coloured pencils to use (2–4).

- Players take turns to colour any section with one of the available colours.
- Game continues until one of the players is forced to colour a section next to a section of the same colour.
  This player is the loser.

Gameboard

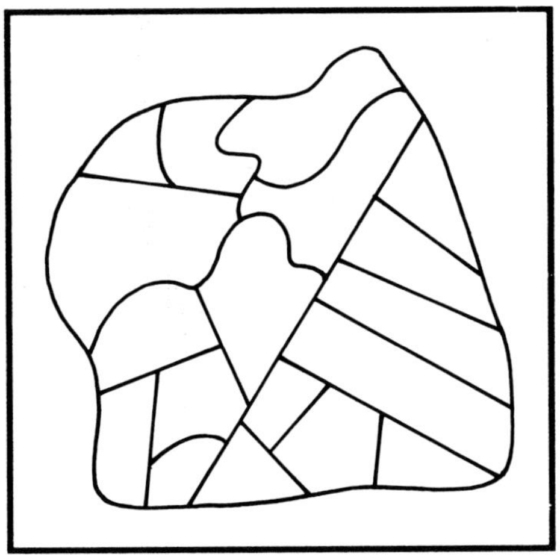

Sample Play

(using 3 pencils)

2

COLOUR-IN

Aim

To be the last player able to colour a section. No section can be coloured the same colour as the section next to it.

Number of players

2

Materials

Gameboard (Worksheet 3), four coloured pencils.

Play

- Players take turns to colour any section with any of the pencils.
- Game continues until one of the players is forced to colour a section that is next to a section of the same colour.
  This player is the loser.

Gameboard

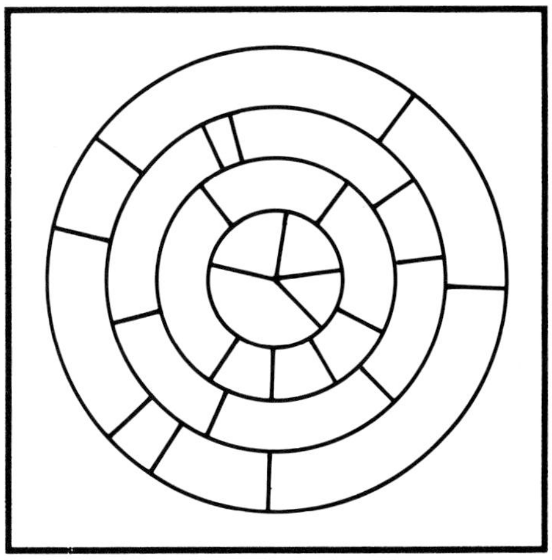

Sample Play

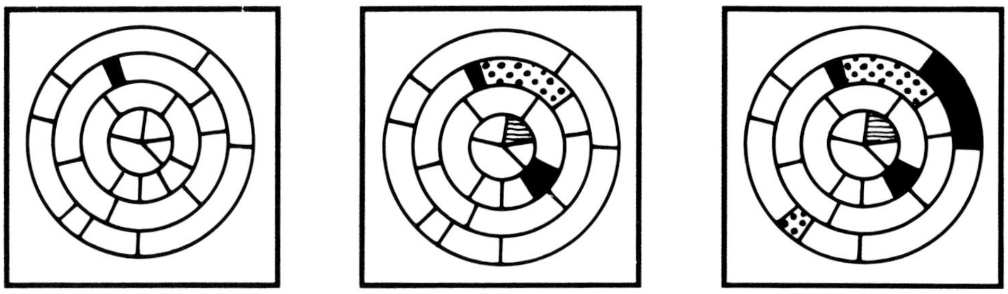

3

GAMEBOARD

(Colour-in)

4

RAT RACE

Aim

To draw three holes, one in each wall, that form a straight line for the rat to get through to the cheese.

Number of players

2

Materials

Gameboard (Worksheet 5), one pencil for each player (different colours).

Play

- Players take turns to draw their mark (**O** or **X**), one at a time in any vacant square on any wall.
- Game continues until one of the players has formed a straight line of three **O**s or **X**s, one in each wall.
  This player is the winner.

Gameboard

Sample Play

Variation – the opening player's first move may be restricted, e.g. the first hole may not be drawn on the central square on any wall.

5

GAMEBOARD

(Rat race)

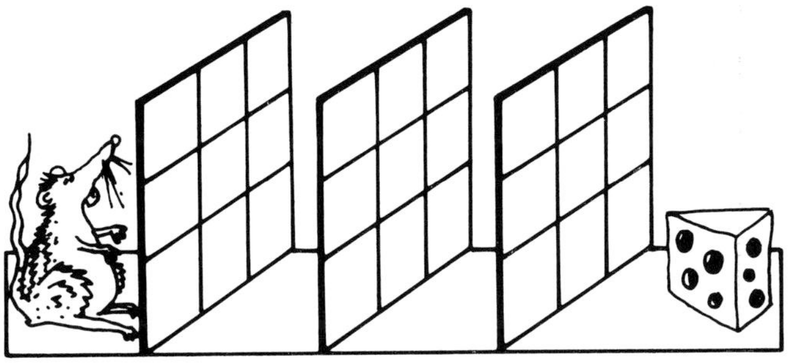

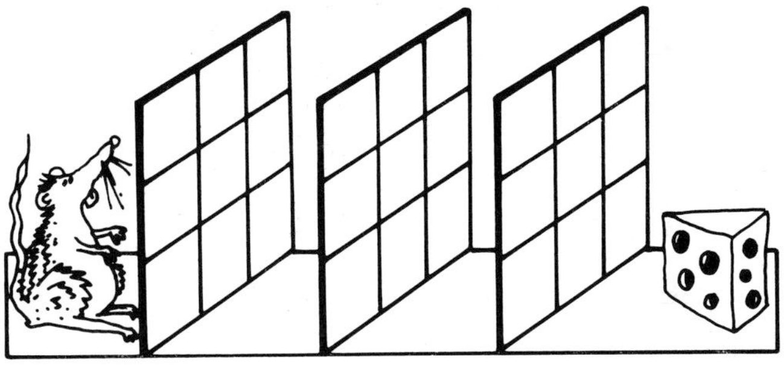

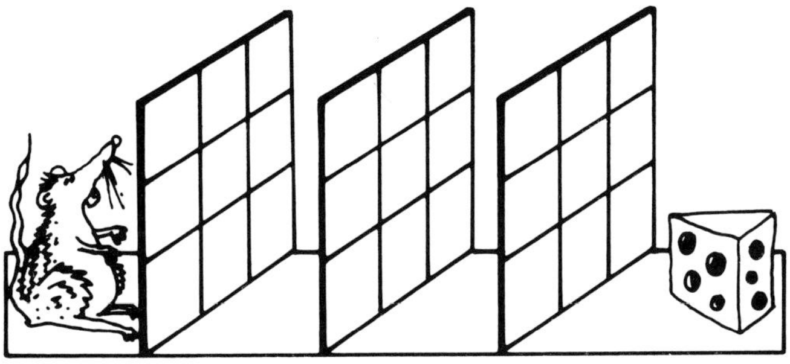

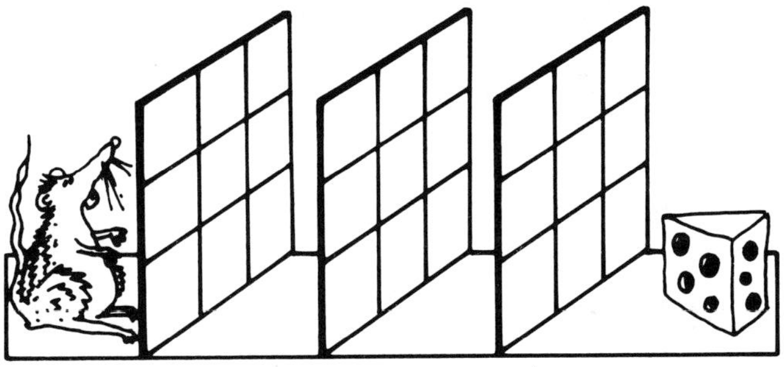

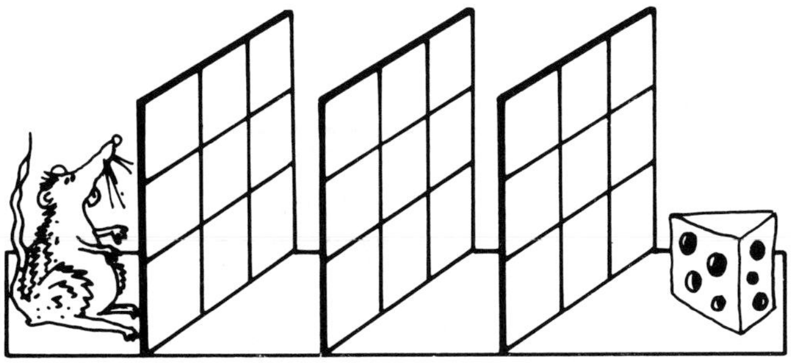

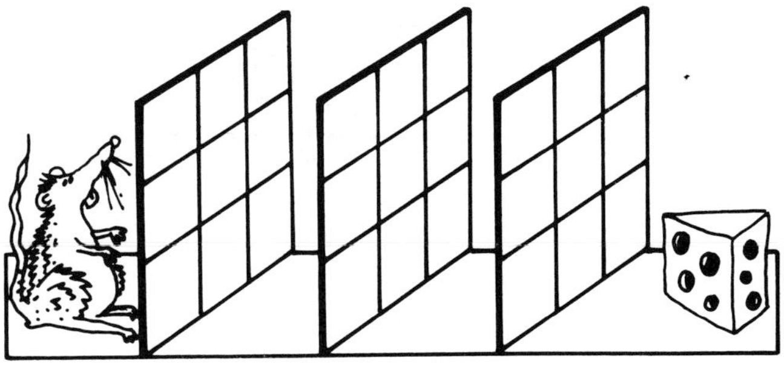

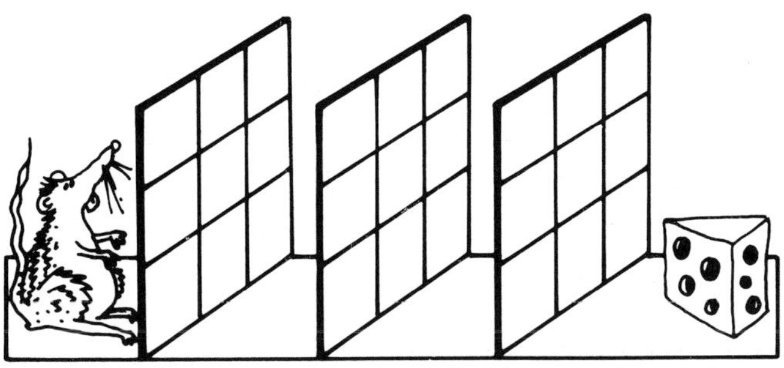

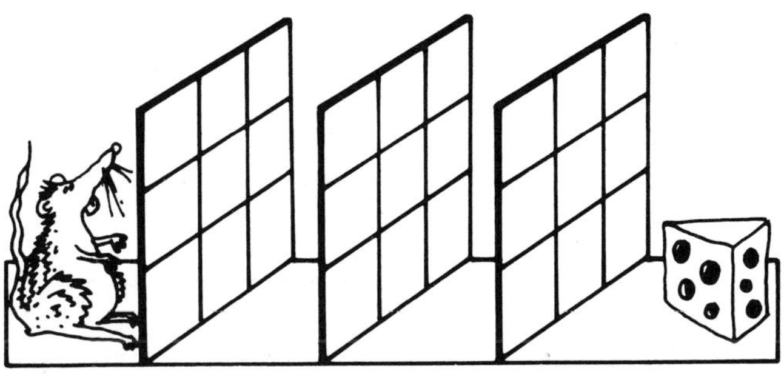

6 FOUR IN A ROW

Aim

To form a row of four marks (horizontally, vertically or diagonally).

Number of players

2

Materials

Gameboard (Worksheet 7), one pencil for each player.

Play

- First player places a mark (**O** or **X**) in any square.
- Second player places a mark in any square, horizontally, vertically or diagonally next to the first player's mark.
- Game continues with players taking turns to place marks on the gameboard, so they are next to one of the earlier marks.
- Game continues until one of the players has made a line of four **O**s or **X**s (horizontally, vertically or diagonally). This player is the winner.

Gameboard

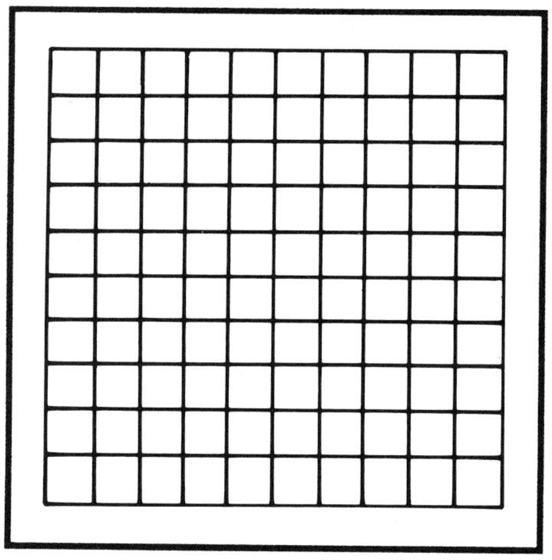

Sample Play

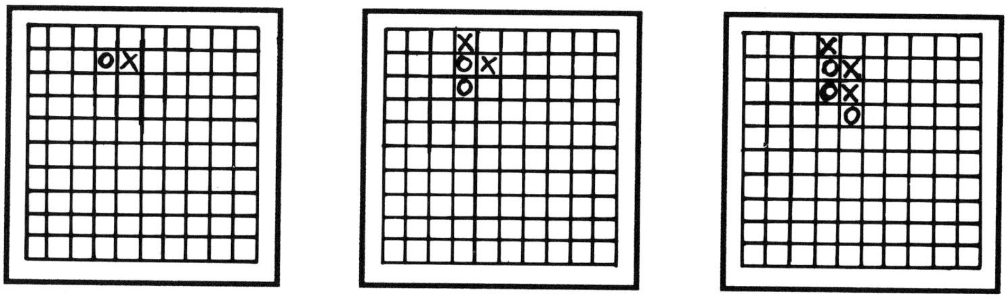

Variation – try to make a line of five or more marks
– allow only horizontal or vertical lines to win
– introduce a third player (use a third symbol or each colour squares with a different coloured pencil).

7

GAMEBOARD

(Four in a row)

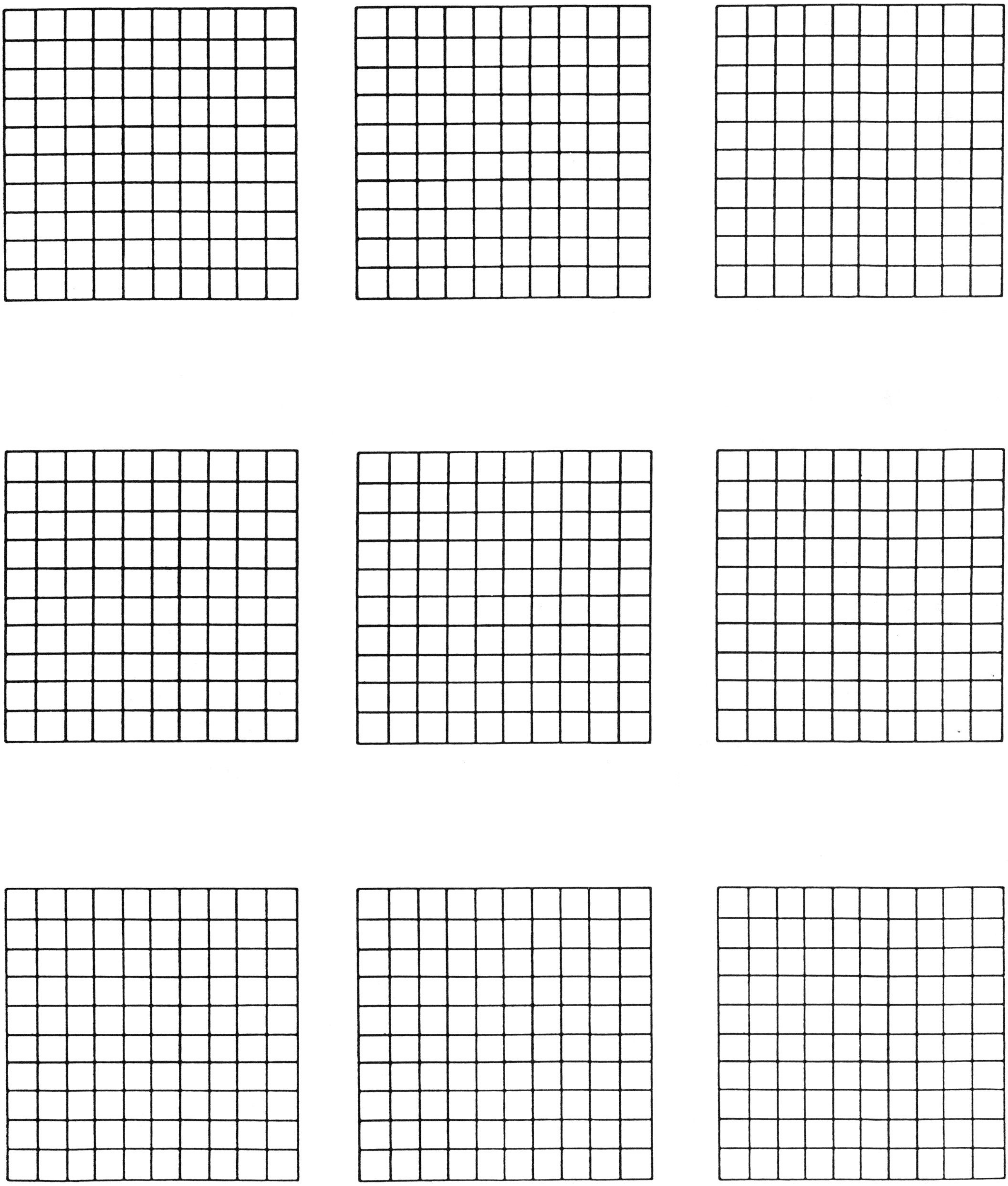

8 GO BANG!

Aim

To form a line of five marks (horizontally or vertically).

Number of players

2

Materials

Gameboard (Worksheet 9), one pencil for each player (different colours).

Play

- Players take turns to draw their mark (**O** or **X**) in any empty square.
- Game continues until one of the players has formed a line of five **O**s or **X**s.
  This player is the winner. (Note – a line of more than five marks is acceptable.)

Gameboard

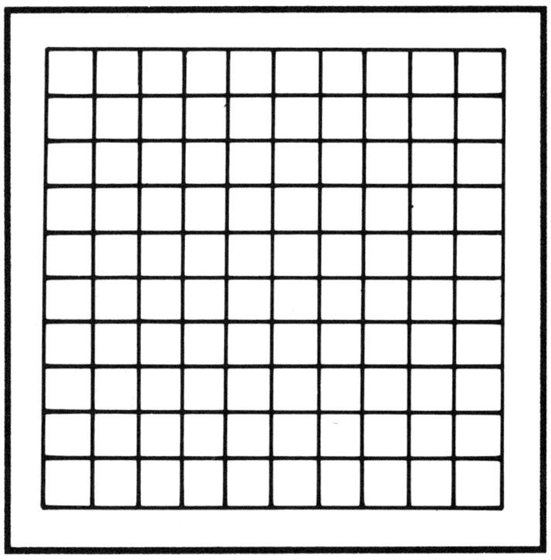

Sample Play

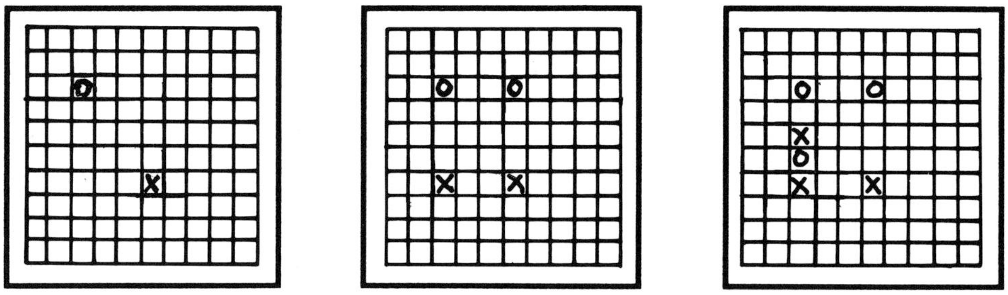

Variation – the winning move must be a line of exactly five marks.

GAMEBOARD

(Go bang)

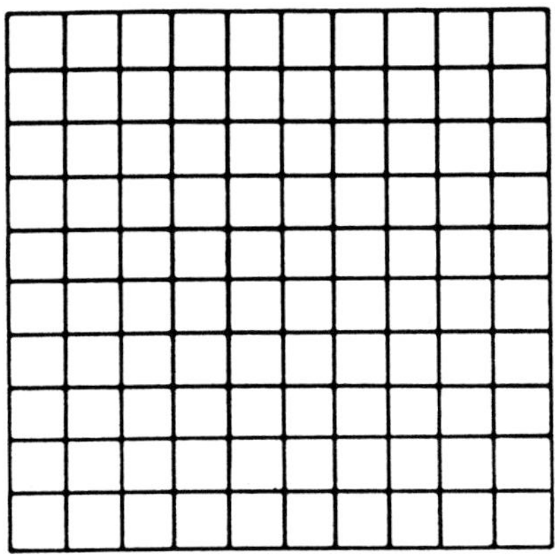
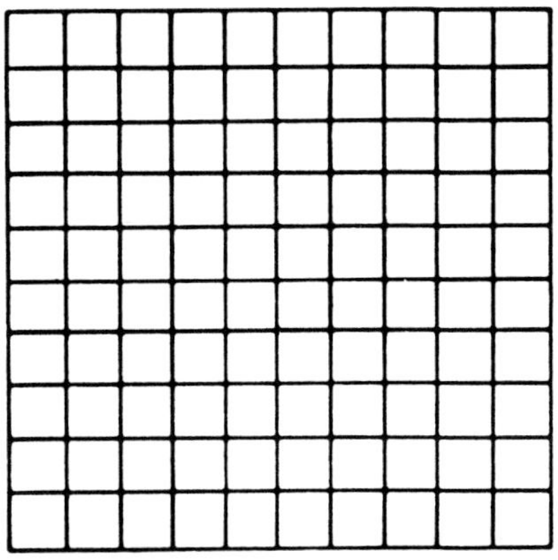
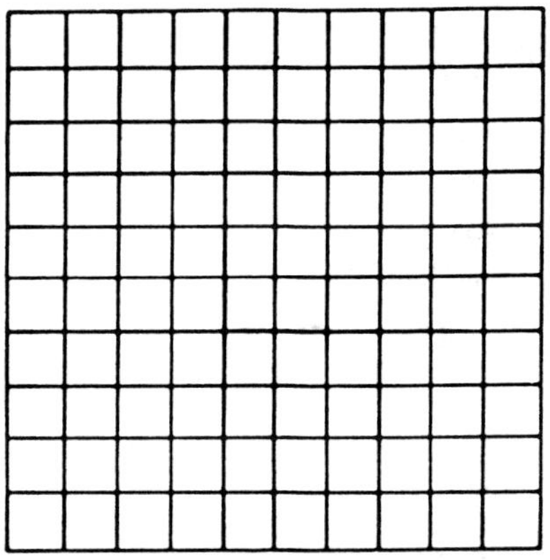
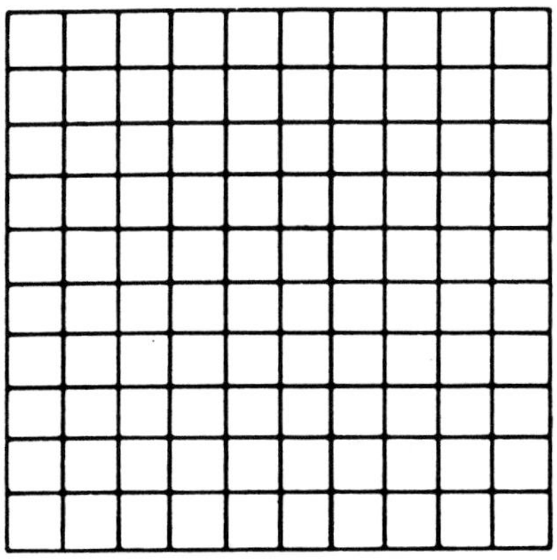
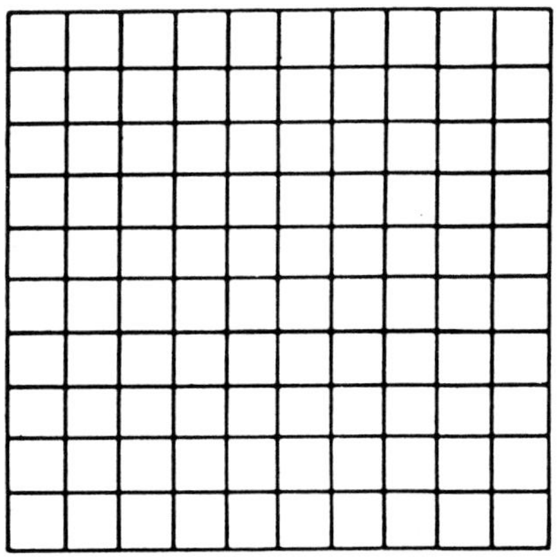
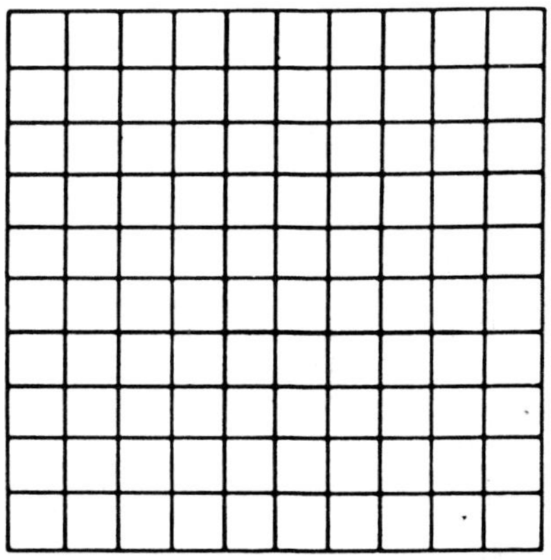
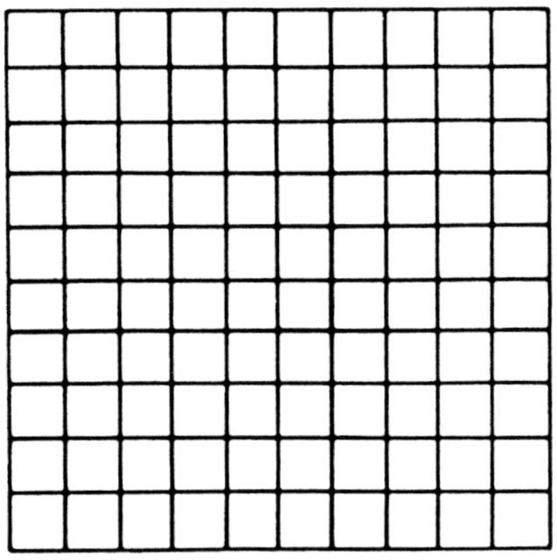
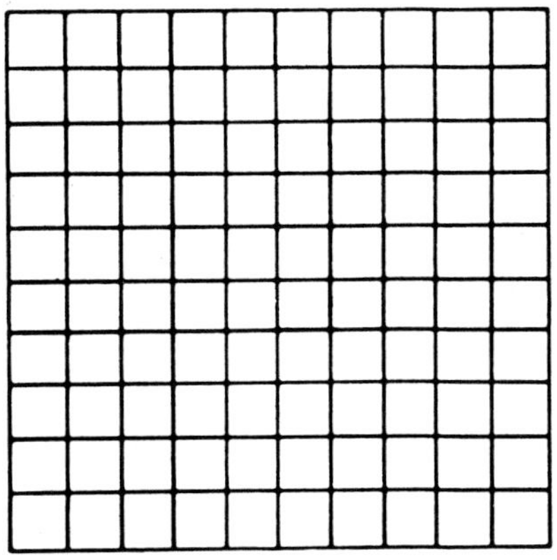
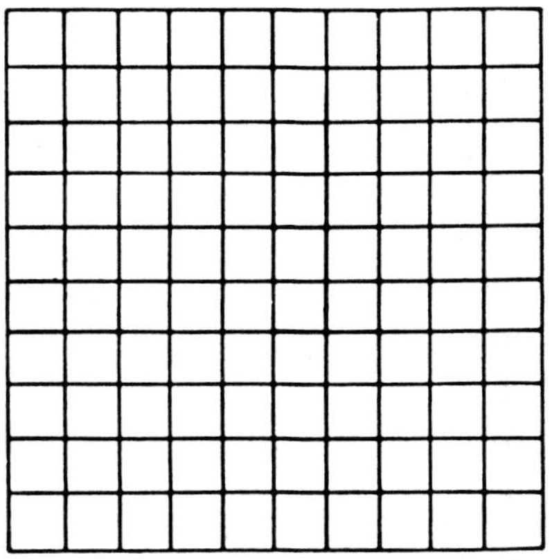

SIM

Aim

Not to draw a triangle.

Number of players

2

Materials

Paper, one pencil for each player (different colours).

Play

Starter: mark six dots on the paper (see 'Gameboard').

- Players take turns to draw a line joining any two dots.
- Game continues until one of the players is forced to form a triangle, made up of three sides of his or her colour. (Note – the corners of the triangle must be three of the original six dots.)
  This player is the loser. (Note – only one line may connect any two points.)

Gameboard

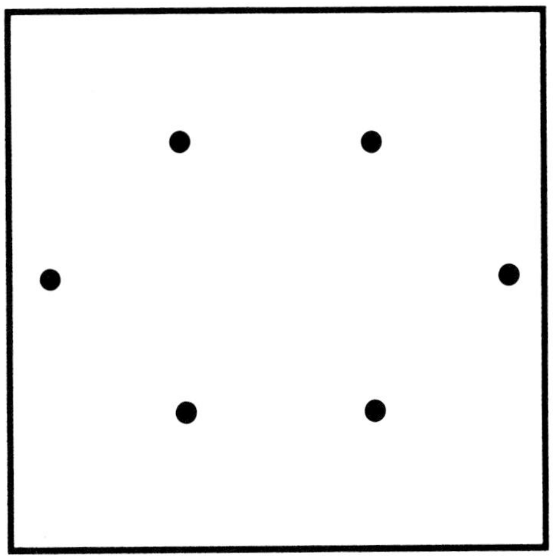

Sample Play

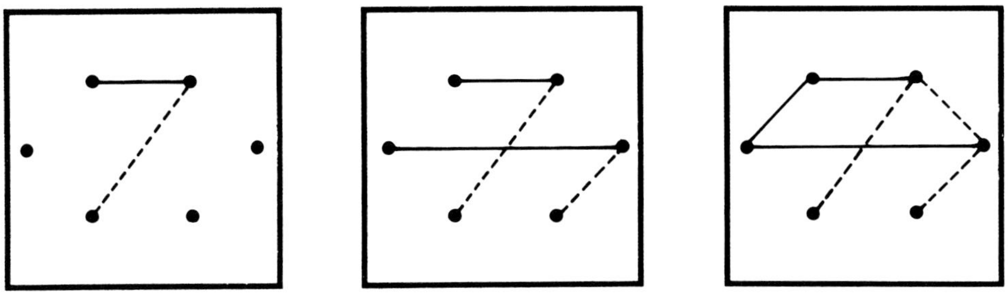

11

SPROUTS

Aim

To make the last connection.

Number of players

2 or 3

Materials

Paper, one pencil for each player (different colours).

Play

Starter: mark between 5 and 10 dots anywhere on the paper.

- Players take turns to draw a line connecting any two dots, or join a dot to itself. (Note – no lines may cross, no line may pass through a point, a point may have a maximum of three lines leaving it.)
  On drawing the connection, the player marks a third point anywhere along the line.
- Game continues until no more connections can be drawn.
  The winner is the last player to make a connection.

Gameboard

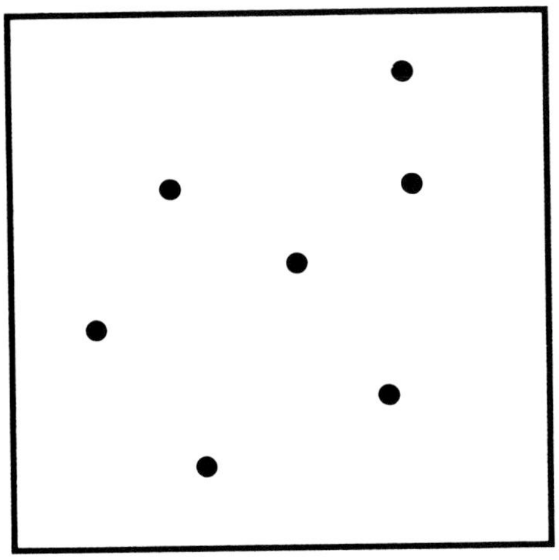

Sample Play

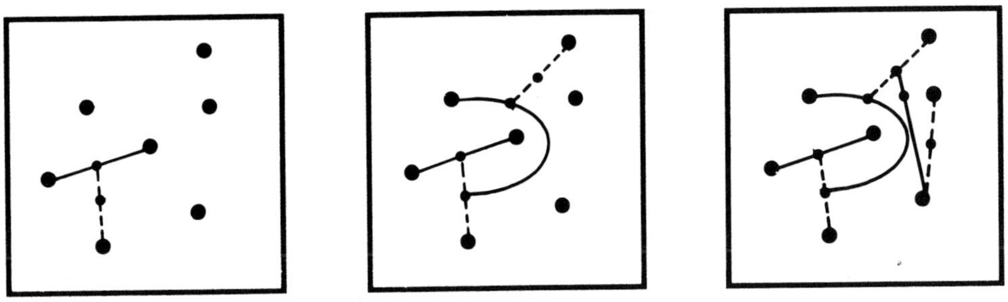

BLACK

Aim

To make a path leading into the 'Black' (or to make the last possible move).

Number of players

2

Materials

Gameboard (Worksheet 13), one pencil for each player.

Play

- Players take turns to draw one of the three possible shapes to make a path into the next horizontal or vertical square. (Note – the path is the space between the curved lines).
- Game continues with players trying to lead the path into the black box. (Note – if a player is forced to lead the path off the gameboard, then he or she loses.)
- Players may win if:
  – they lead the path into the 'Black'
  – their opponent cannot make a move
  – their opponent leads the path off the gameboard.

Gameboard

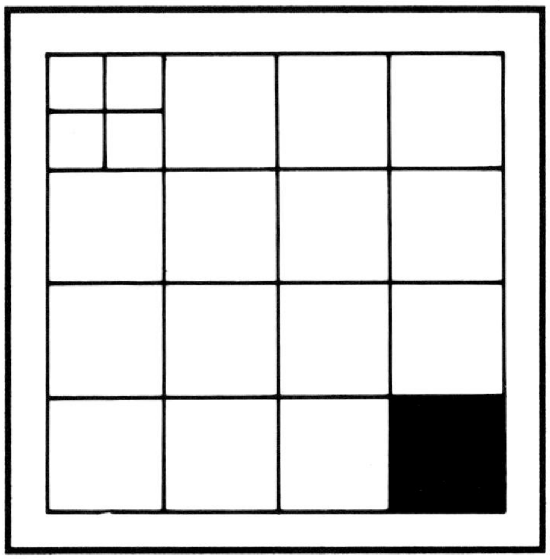

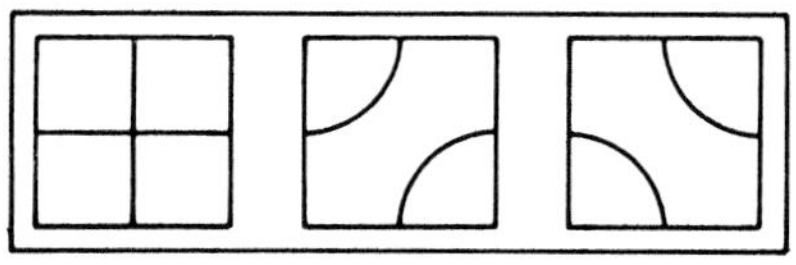

Sample Play

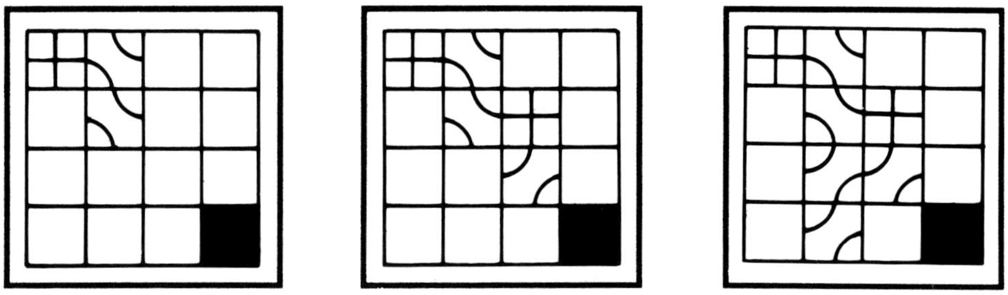

Variation – the size and shape of the gameboard may be varied.

13

GAMEBOARD

(Black)

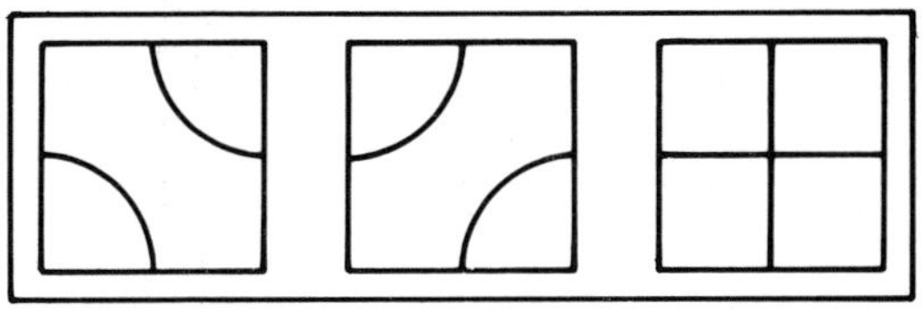

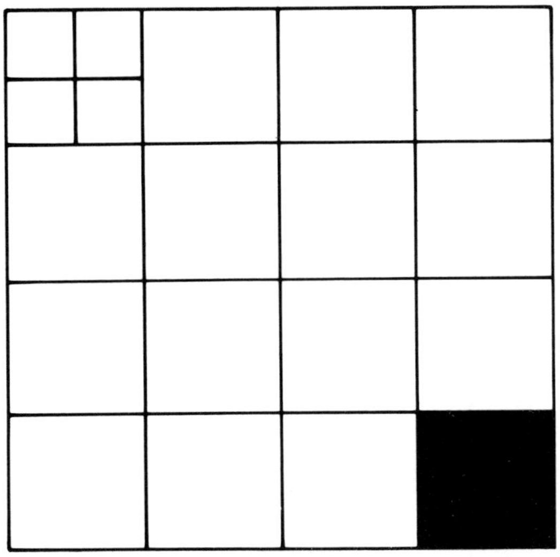

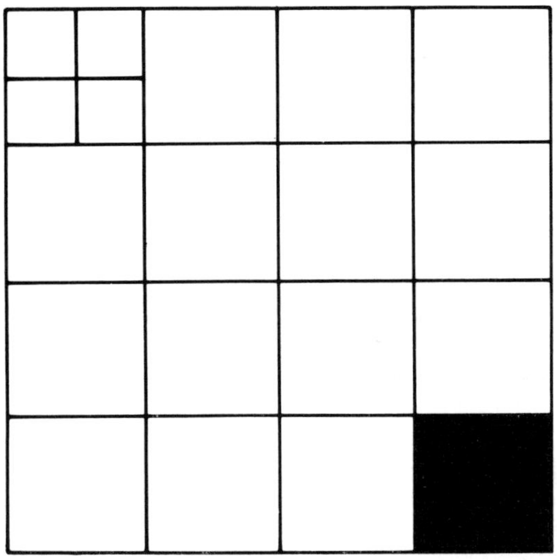

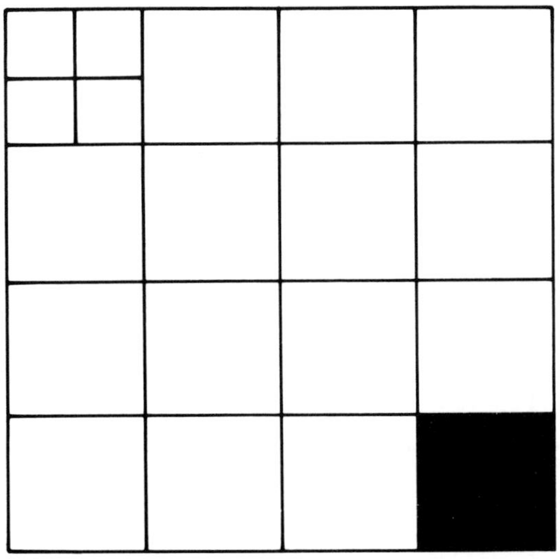

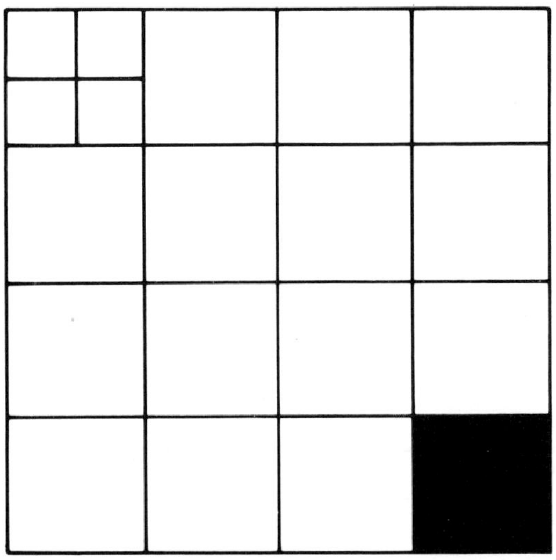

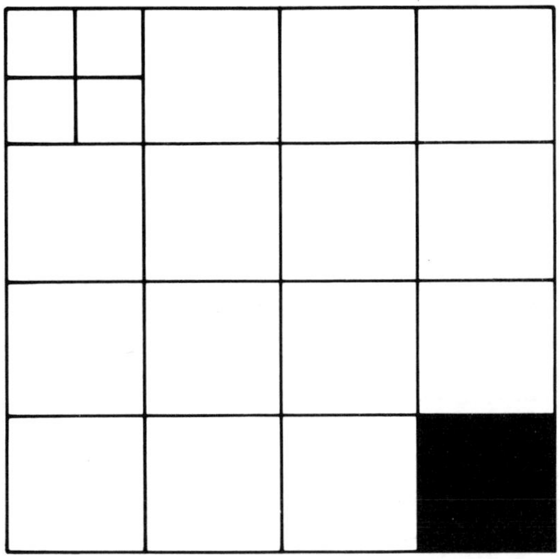

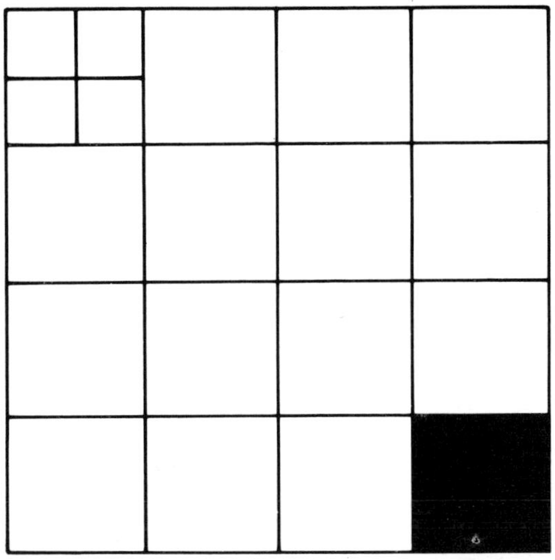

14

KAYLES GAME

Aim

To claim the last X.

Number of players

2, 3 or 4

Materials

Gameboard (Worksheet 15), one pencil for each player (different colours).

Play

- Players take turns to draw a line through any one or two Xs which are next to each other in any single horizontal or vertical row.
- Game continues until one of the players marks the last X. This player is the winner.

Gameboard

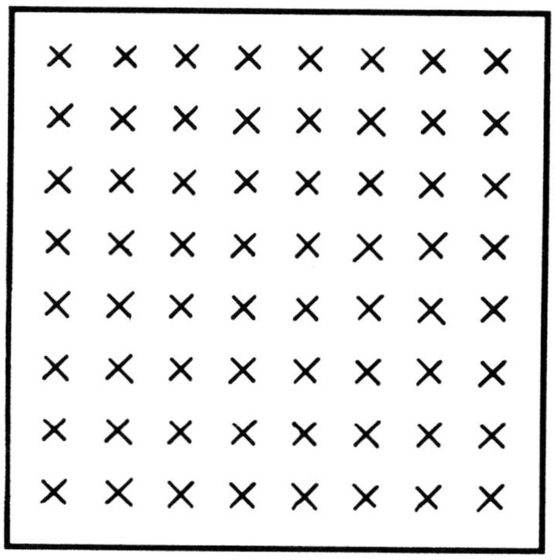

Sample Play

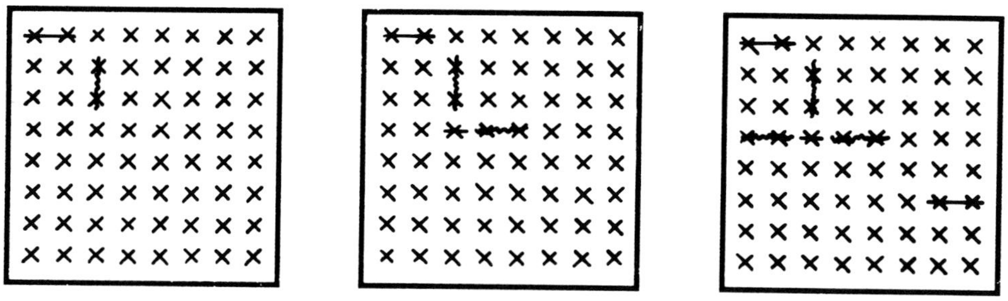

Variation – the player who marks the last X loses.

GAMEBOARD

(Kayles game)

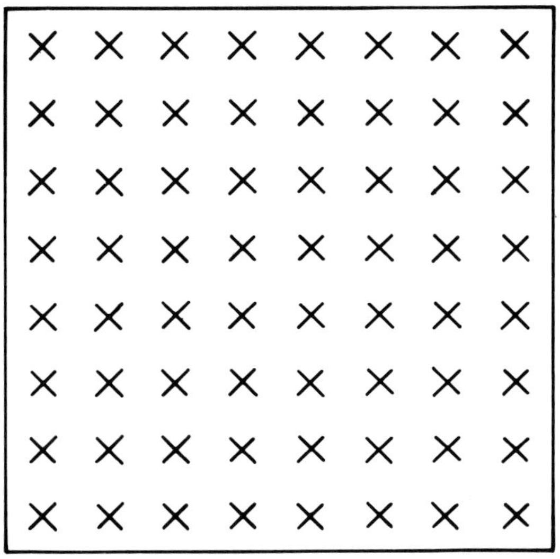

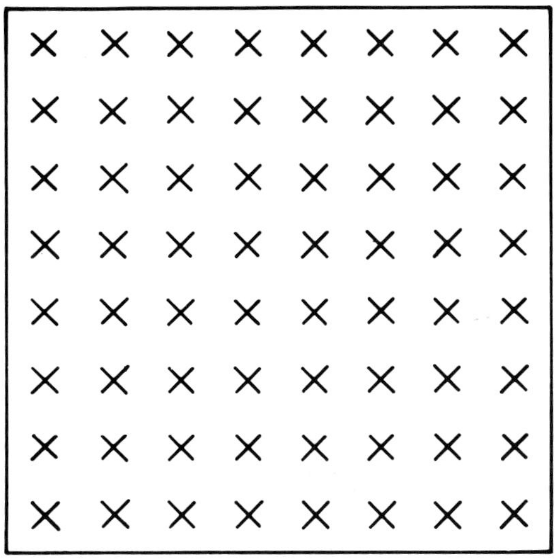

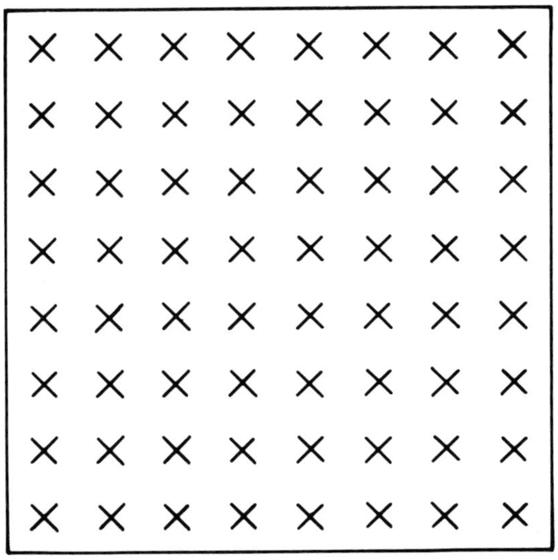

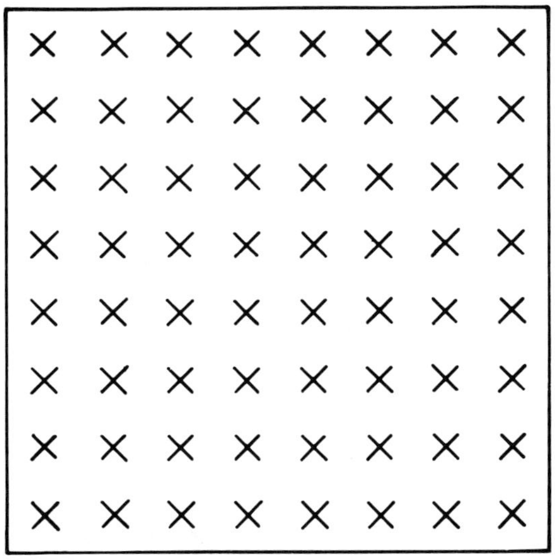

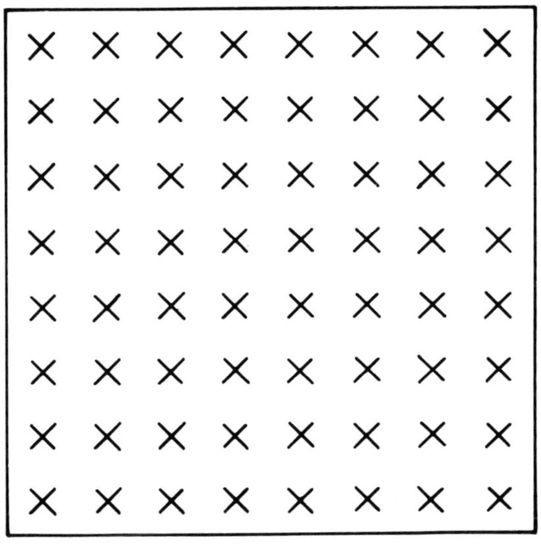

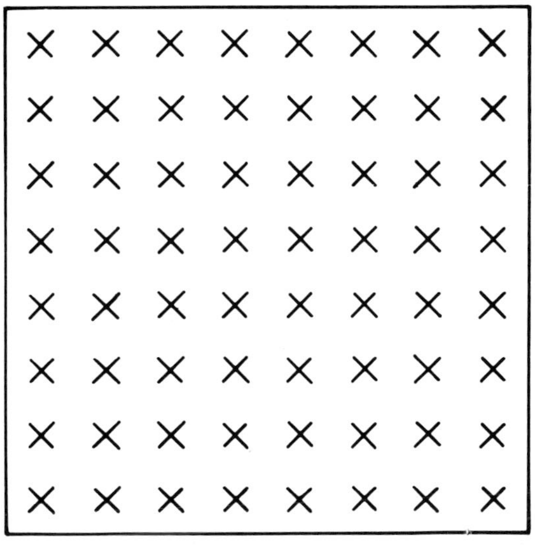

CROSS-O

Aim

Not to claim the X.

Number of players

2, 3 or 4

Materials

Gameboard (Worksheet 17), one pencil for each player (different colours).

Play

- Players take turns to draw a straight line through a row of any number of horizontal or vertical noughts.
- Game continues until one of the players is forced to mark the X. This player is the loser.

Gameboard

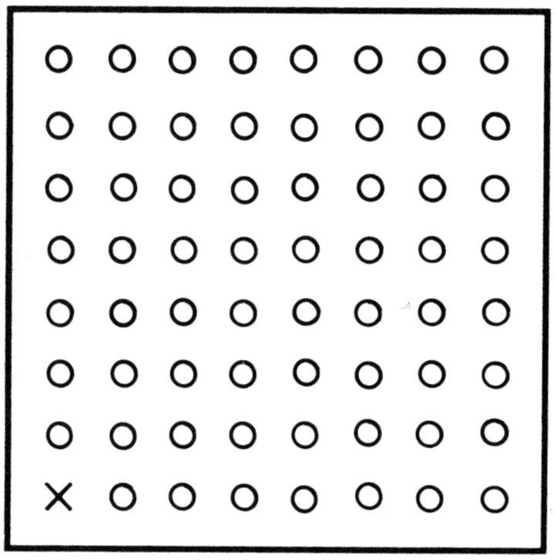

Sample Play

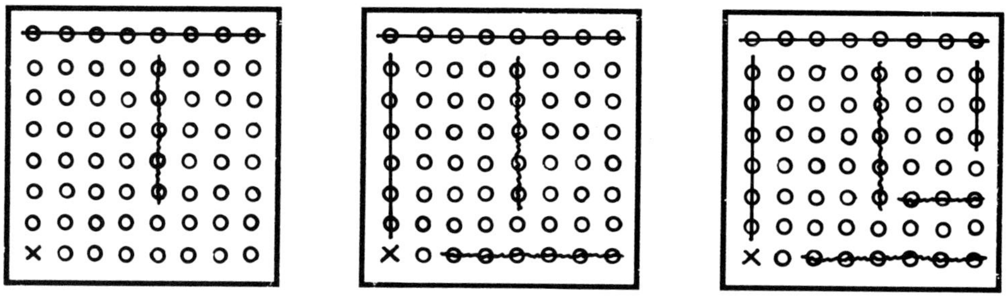

GAMEBOARD

(Cross-O)

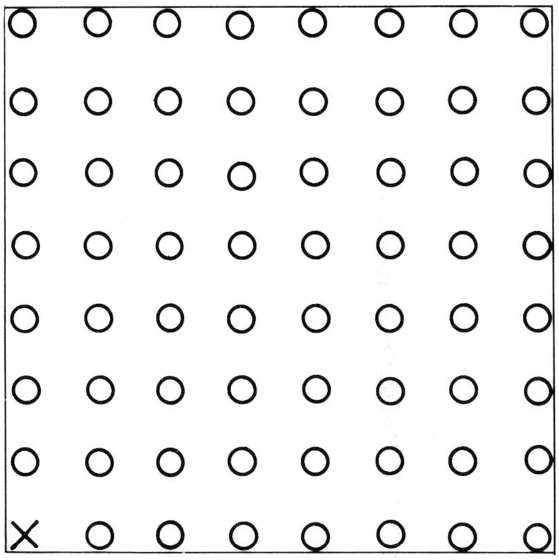

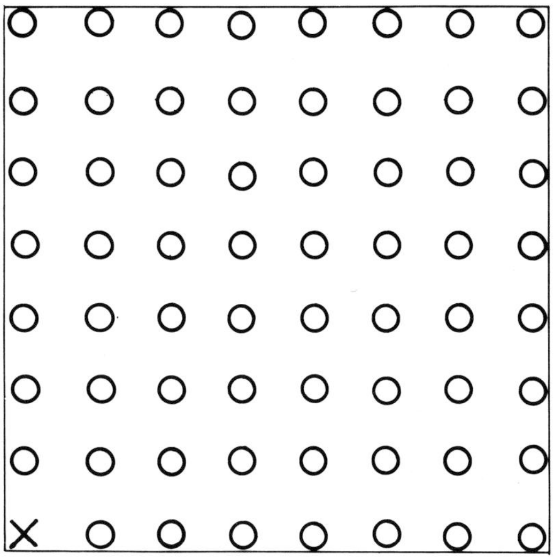

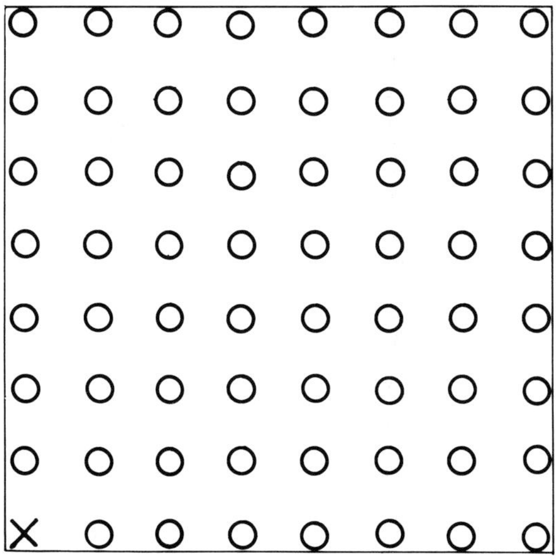

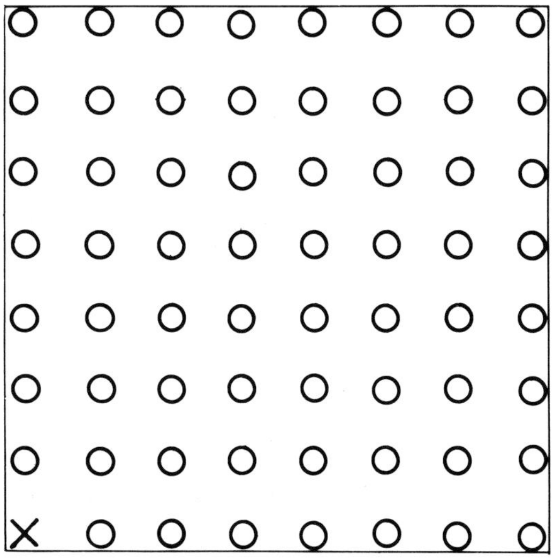

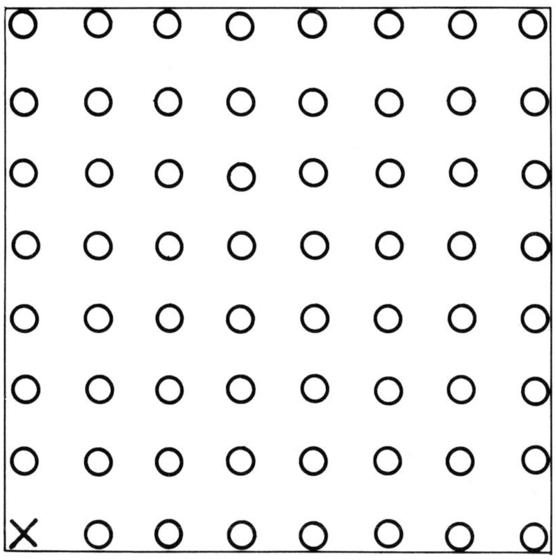

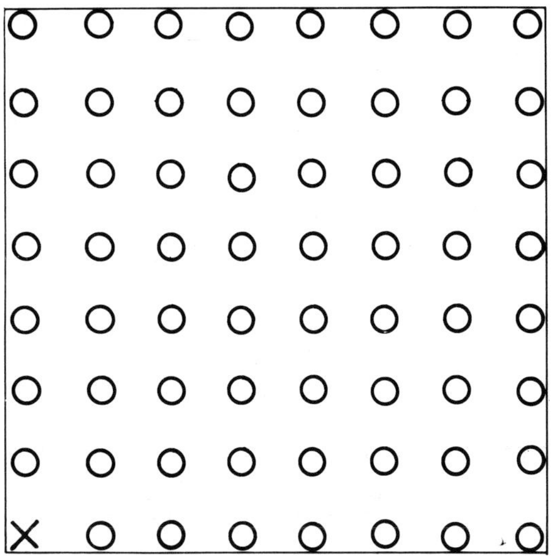

18 CHOPSTICKS

Aim

To claim the last 'chopstick' segment.

Number of players

2 or 3

Materials

Gameboard (Worksheet 19), one pencil for each player (different colours).

Play

- Players take turns to colour any number of connected sections of any one chopstick.
- Game continues until one of the players colours the last section. This player is the winner.

Gameboard

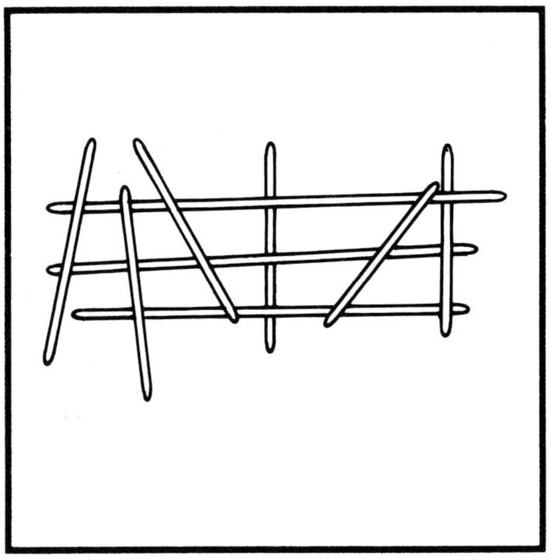

Sample Play

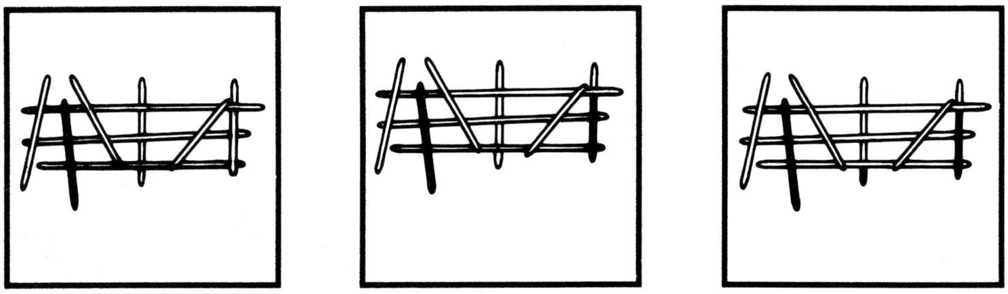

Variation – players may further divide the chopsticks into smaller sections, using a black pen
– players may be restricted to claiming only one or two connected sections.

GAMEBOARD

(Chopsticks)

20 SUBDIVISION

Aim

To claim the last block of land by placing the marker in the last subdivision segment.

Number of players

2 or 3

Materials

Paper, one pencil for each player (different colours).

Play

Starter: draw the block of land.
Players then take turns to draw a line anywhere across the block, ending either at the border or on any other line – draw four lines each. (See 'Gameboard'.)

- Players take turns to colour in one, two or three of the sections.
- Game continues until one of the players colours in the last section of land. This player is the winner.

Gameboard

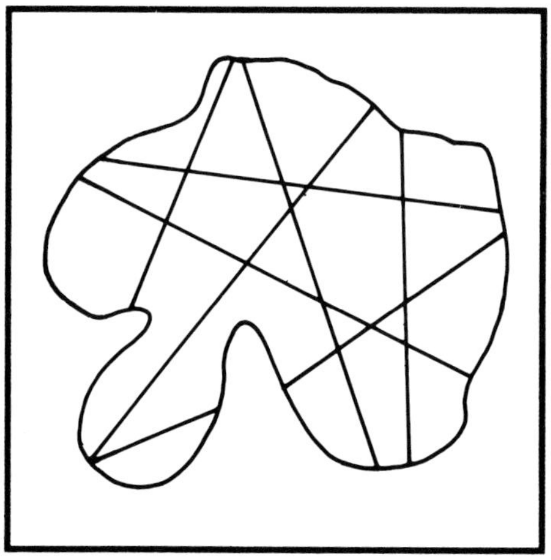

Sample Play

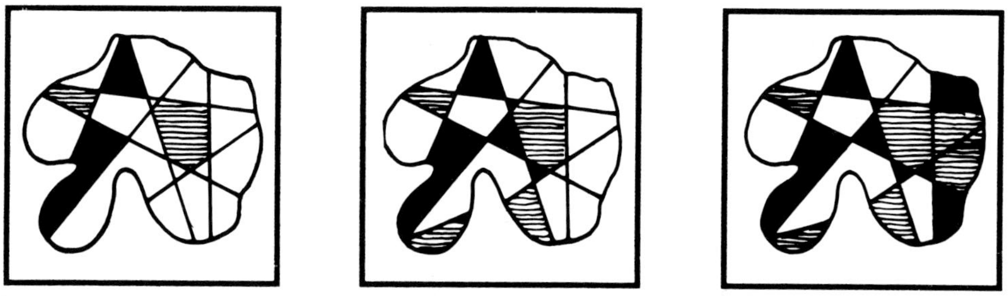

Variation – the number of lines drawn across the block of land may be varied
– the player who colours the last block loses.

21

POISON

Aim

Not to pick up the 'poison' counter.

Number of players

2

Materials

Nine counters and a 'poison' counter.

Play

Starter: arrange counters in formation (see 'starting position').

- Players take turns to pick up one, two or three counters from the left of the line.
- Game continues until one of the players is forced to pick up the 'poison' counter.
  This player is the loser.

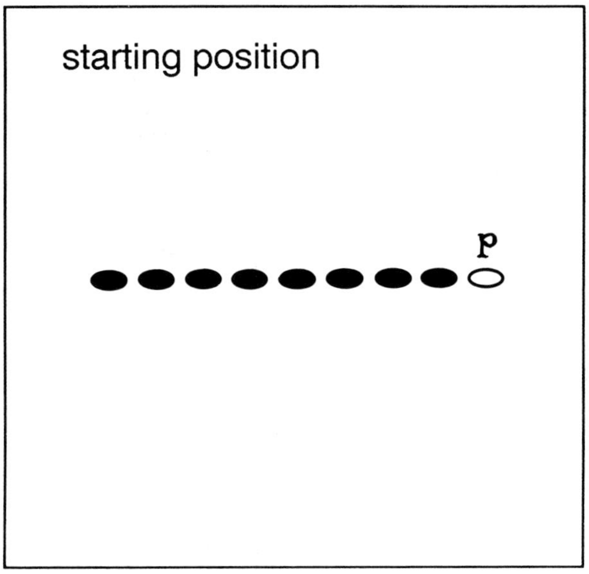

Variation – pick up more or fewer counters in each turn
– play with three players.

TRIPLI-COLOUR

Aim

To be the last player able to place a counter so that it is not horizontally or vertically next to a counter of the same colour.

Number of players

2

Materials

Gameboard (Worksheet 23), eight counters in each of three colours.

Play

Starter: players have four each of each colour counter (twelve counters each).

- Players take turns to place any counter on a dot on the gameboard.
- Game continues until one of the players is forced to place a counter next to a counter of the same colour.
  This player is the loser.
  (Note – a draw occurs if all the dots are covered with counters and there are no counters next to a counter of the same colour.)

Gameboard

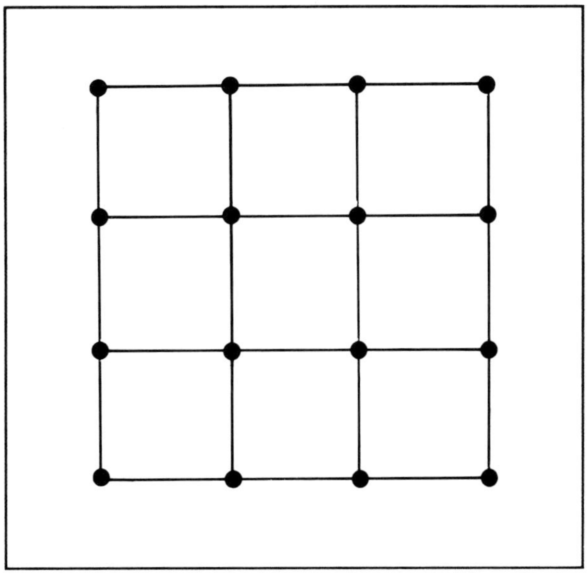

Variation – play with three players. Each player has four counters of each colour (twelve counters each).

23

GAMEBOARD

(Tripli-colour)

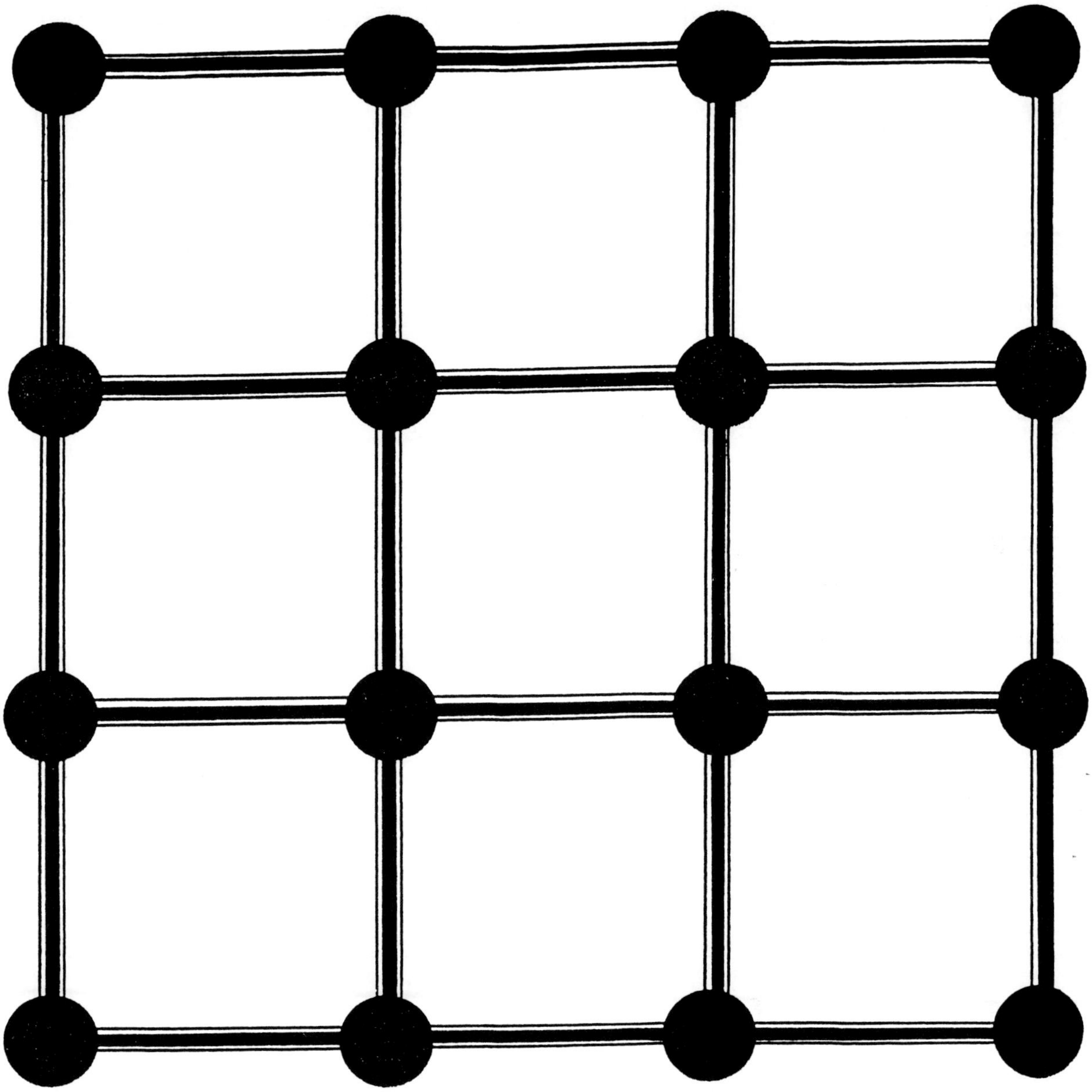

STRATEGY PLUS

Aim

To form a row of three counters (horizontally or vertically).

Number of players

2

Materials

Gameboard (Worksheet 25), four counters for each player (different colours).

Play

Starter: arrange counters (see 'starting position').

- Players take turns to move a counter to a free position next to where it was before.
- Game continues until one of the players has formed a row of three counters.
  This player is the winner.

Gameboard

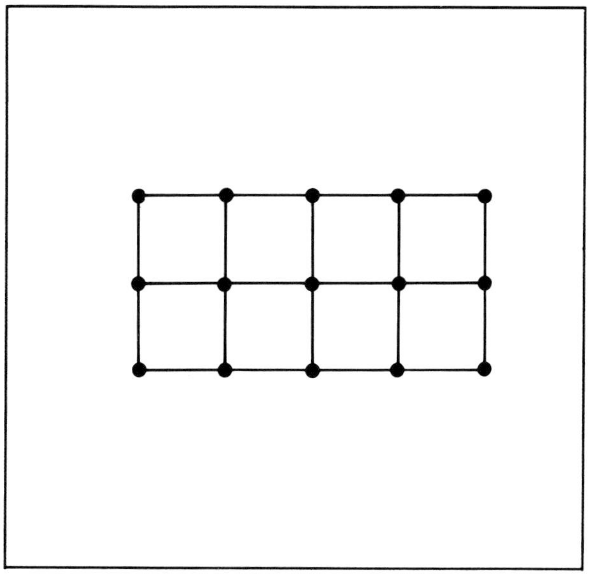

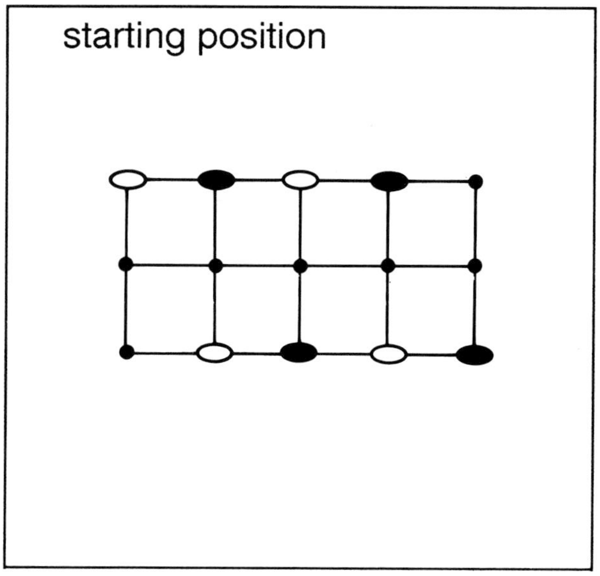

GAMEBOARD

(Strategy plus)

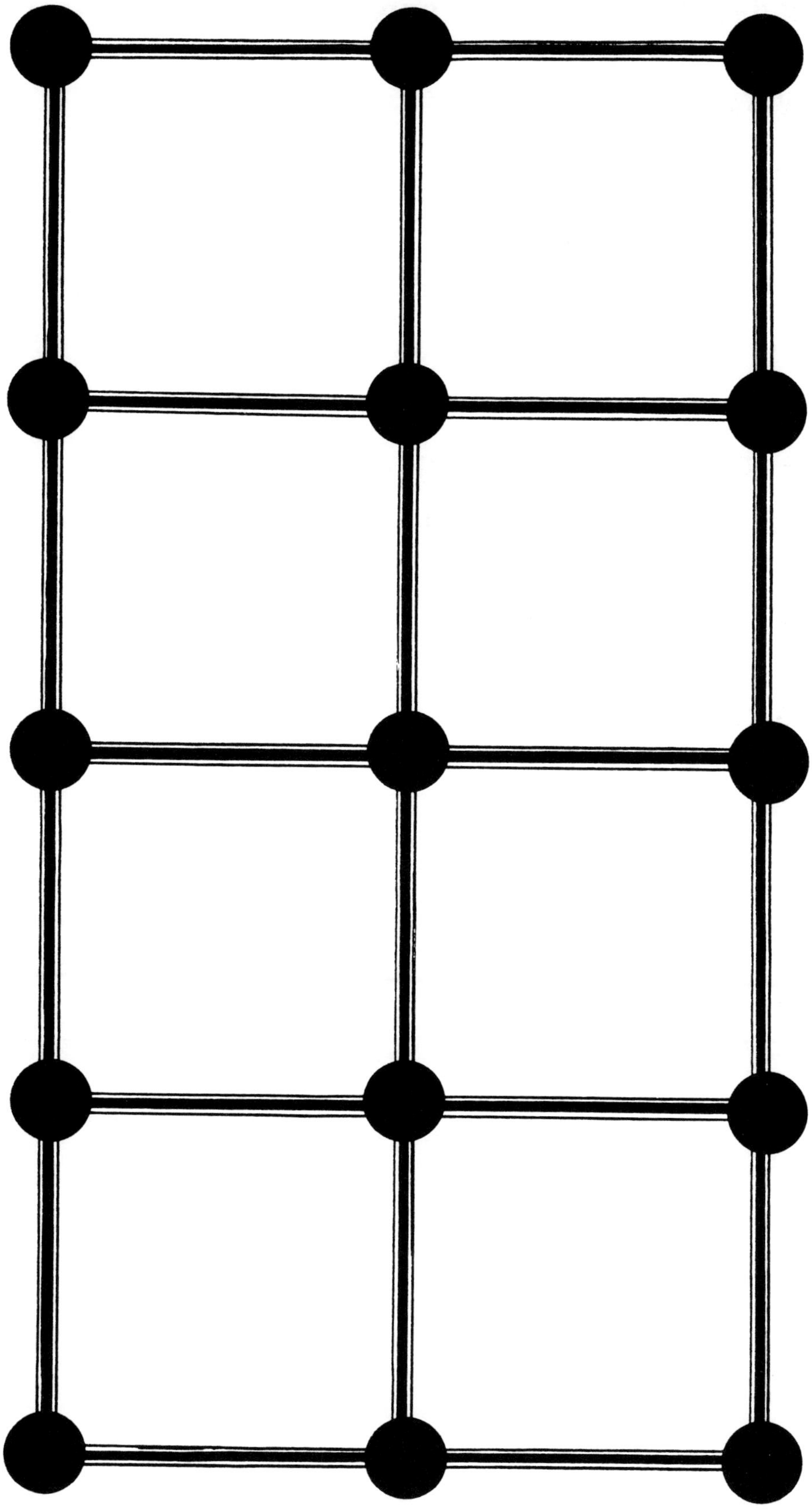

TAC-TICKLE

Aim

To form a row of three counters (horizontally, vertically or diagonally).

Number of players

2

Materials

Gameboard (Worksheet 27), four counters for each player (different colours).

Play

Starter: arrange counters (see 'starting position').

- Players take turns to move a counter to a free position next to where it was before.
- Game continues until one of the players has formed a row of three counters.
  This player is the winner.

Gameboard

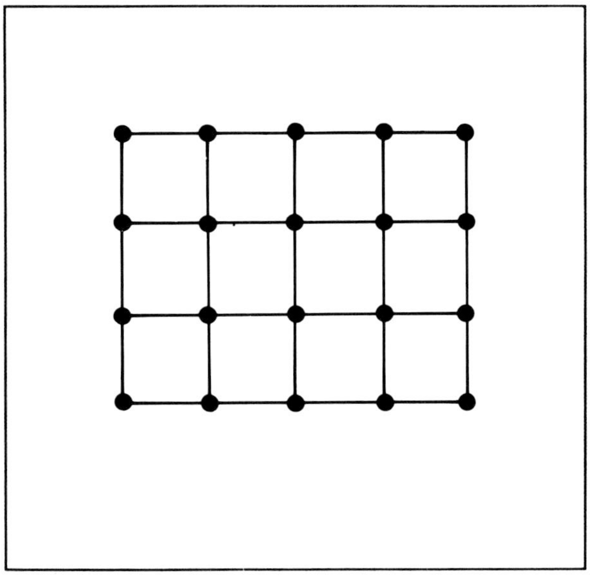

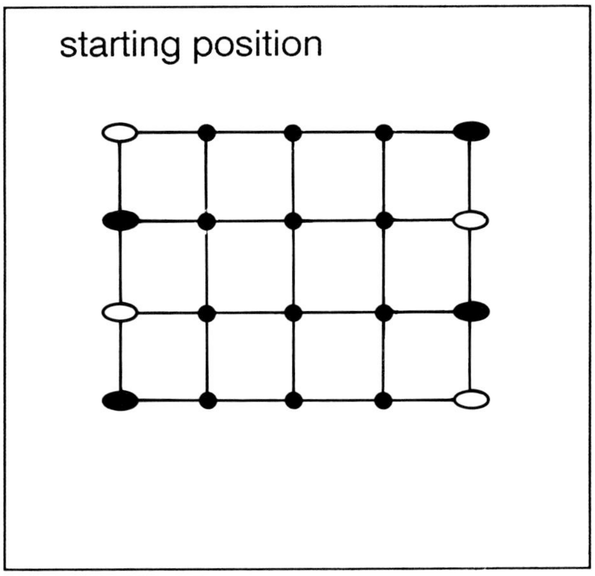

GAMEBOARD

(Tac-tickle)

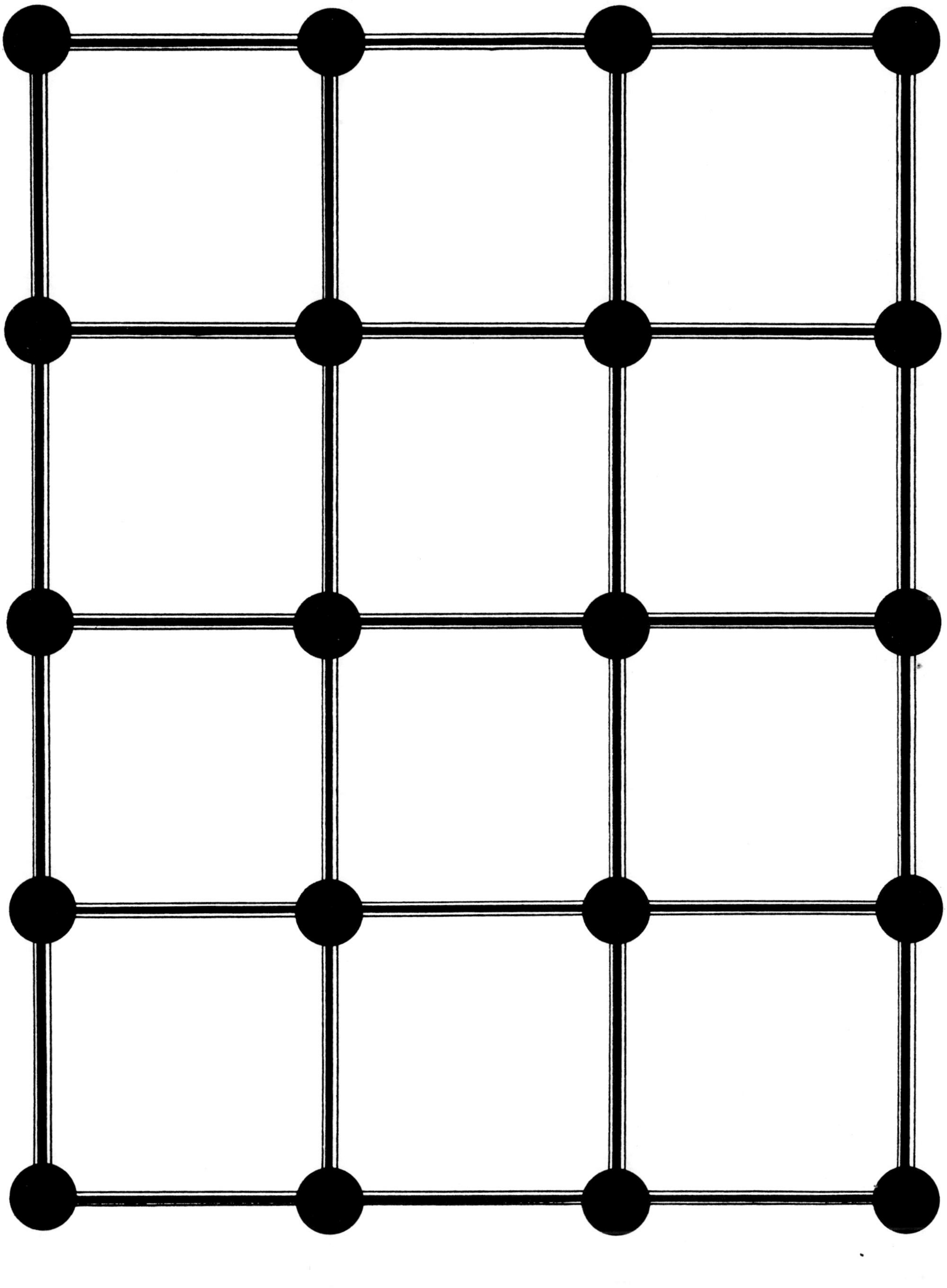

FIVE MEN'S MORRIS

Aim

To win your opponent's counters until he or she has only two counters left. (Players only win an opponent's counter when he or she has made a row of three counters.)

Number of players

2 or 3

Materials

Gameboard (Worksheet 29), five counters for each player (different colours).

Play

Starter: players have their counters in hand.

- Players take turns to place their counters on any circle on the gameboard.
- After placement of all counters, players take turns to move a counter to a position next to where it was before, trying to form a row of three counters.
- On making a row of three counters, the player may take any one of their opponent's counters.
  (Note – once a line of three has been made it cannot be made again.)
- Game continues until one of the players has only two counters left.
  This player is the loser.
  (Note – if a player is blocked, then the game is forfeited.)

Gameboard

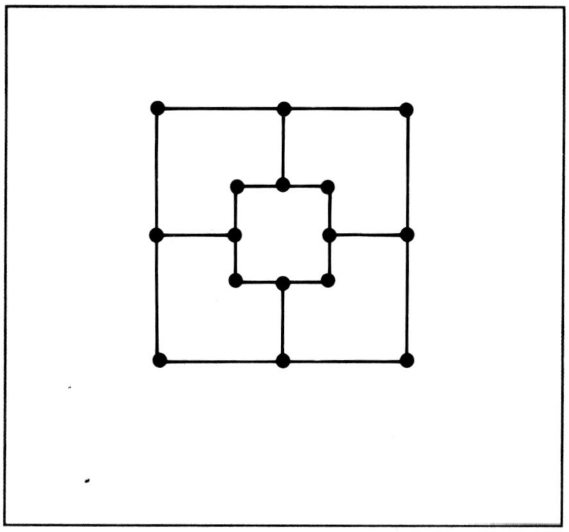

GAMEBOARD

(Five men's morris)

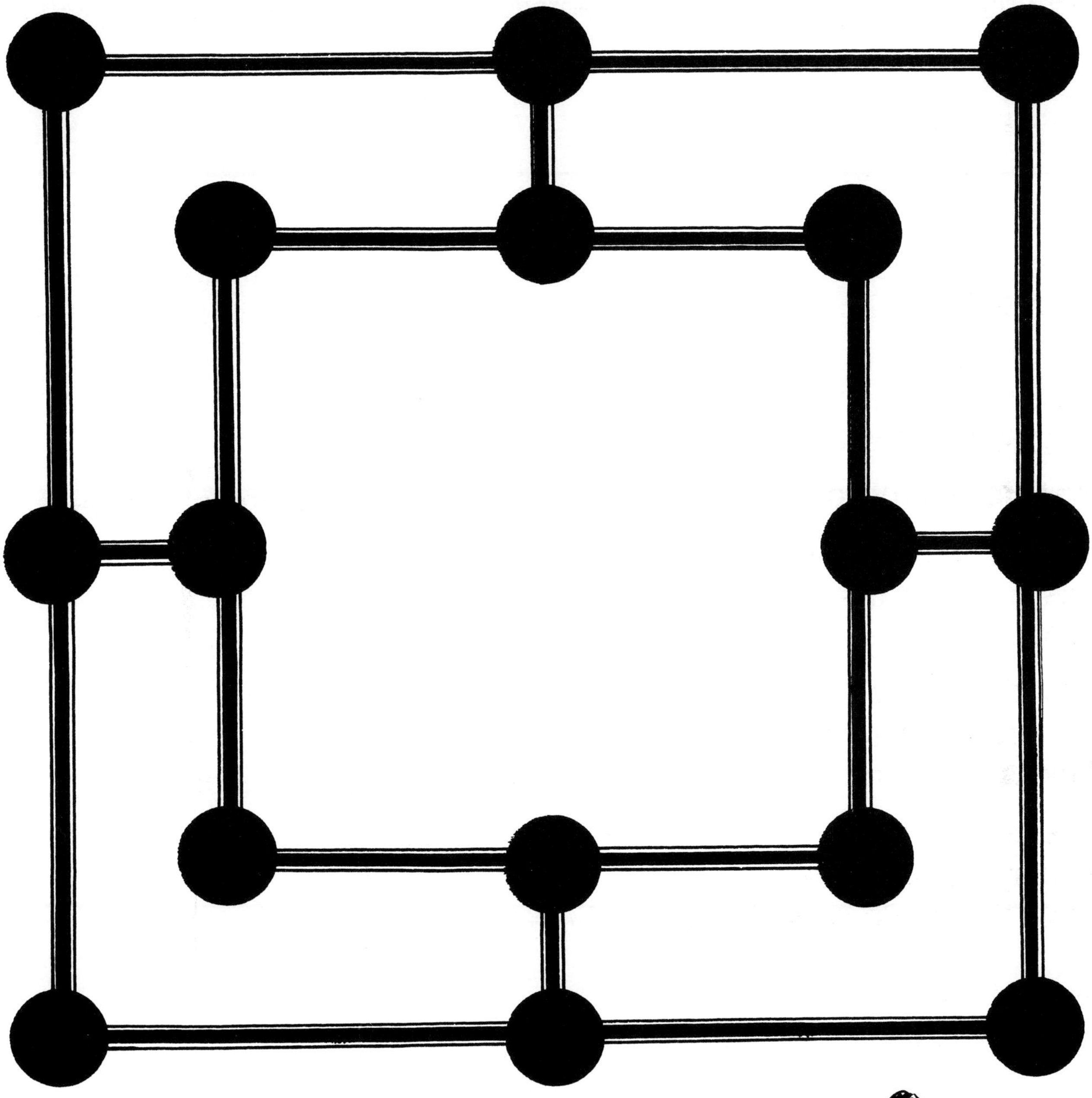

30

Squeeze Between

Aim

To place one of your counters immediately between two opponent's counters (three counters must form a row horizontally, vertically or diagonally).

Number of players

2

Materials

Gameboard (Worksheet 31), two counters for each player (different colours).

Play

Starter: arrange counters (see 'starting position').

- Players take turns to move either of their counters one square, horizontally, vertically or diagonally.
- Game continues until one of the players succeeds in placing a counter between two of the opponent's counters.
  This player is the winner.

Gameboard

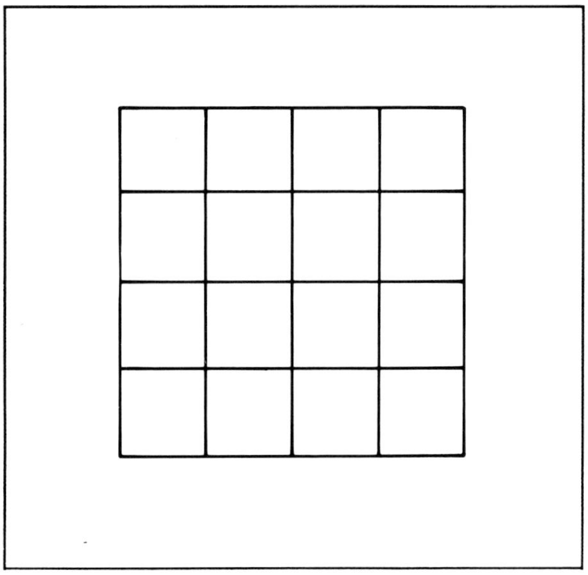

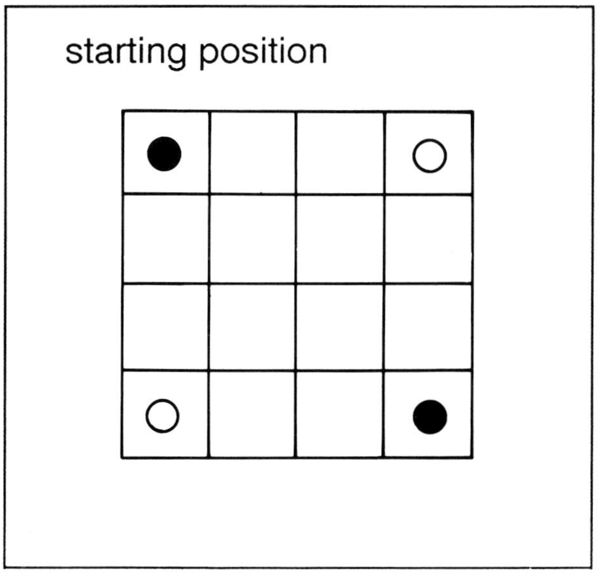

GAMEBOARD

(Squeeze between)

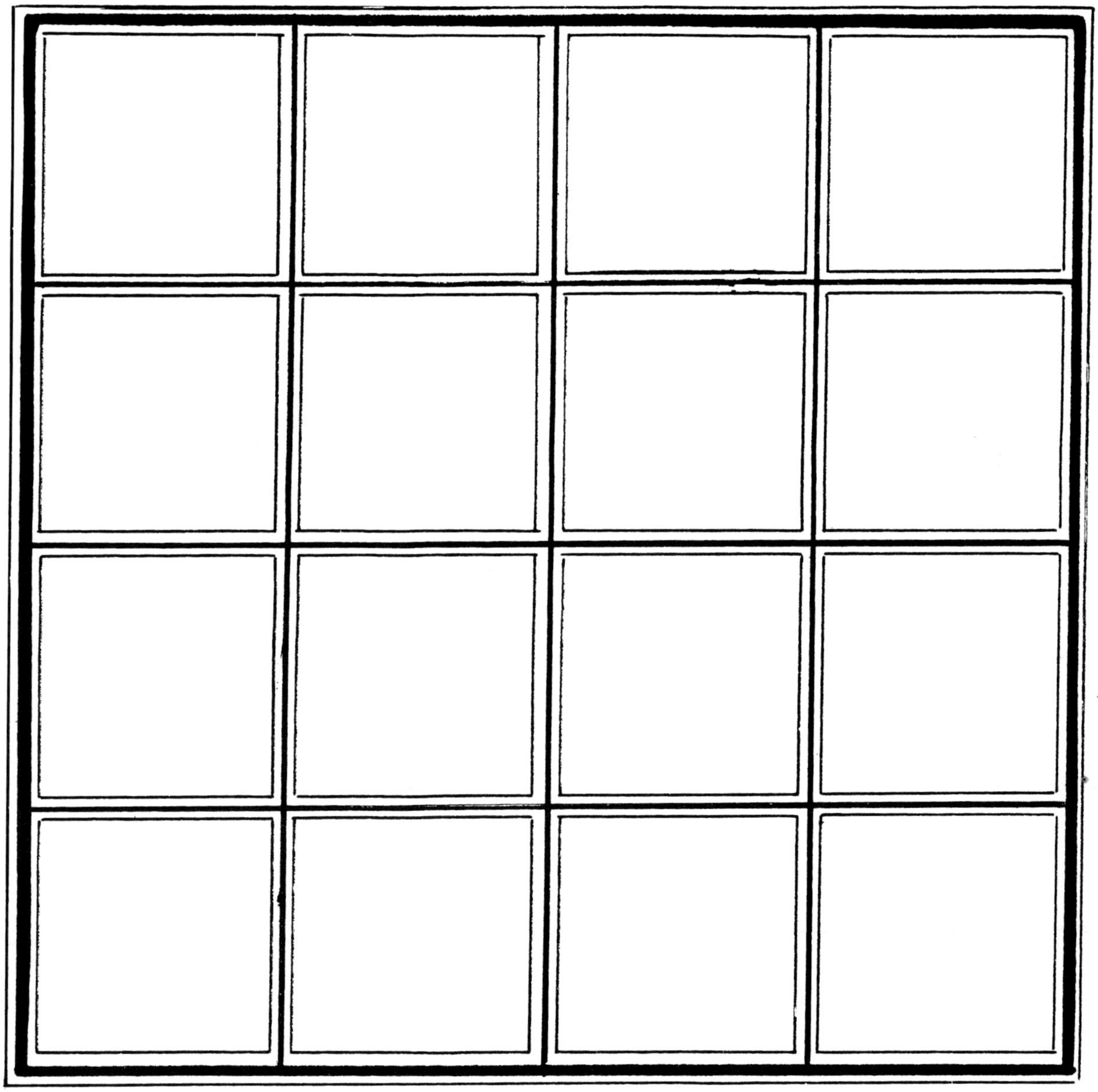

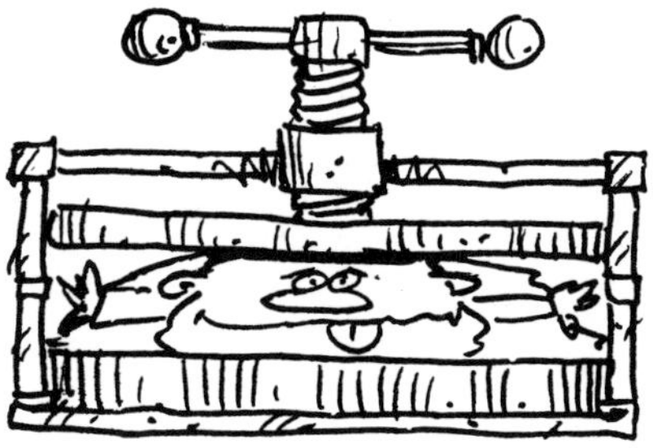

SEVENTEEN CHIPS

Aim

Not to claim the last counter.

Number of players

2 or 3

Materials

Twenty-seven counters, paper.

Play

Starter: draw simple gameboard (see 'Gameboard').
arrange counters in stacks of three on each dot (see 'starting position').

- Players take turns to pick up:
  - the top counter from any single stack **or**
  - two counters from any single stack **or**
  - two which are next to each other in any horizontal or vertical (not diagonal) row of stacks.
- Game continues until one of the players is forced to pick up the last counter.
  This player is the loser.

Gameboard

Variation – winner is the player who picks up the last counter
– use more counters in each stack.

CUBE-O

Aim

Not to claim the last counter.

Number of players

2 or 3

Materials

Seventeen counters.

Play

Starter: spread out the counters.

- Players take turns to pick up any one, two or three counters.
- Game continues until one of the players is forced to pick up the last counter.
  This player is the loser.

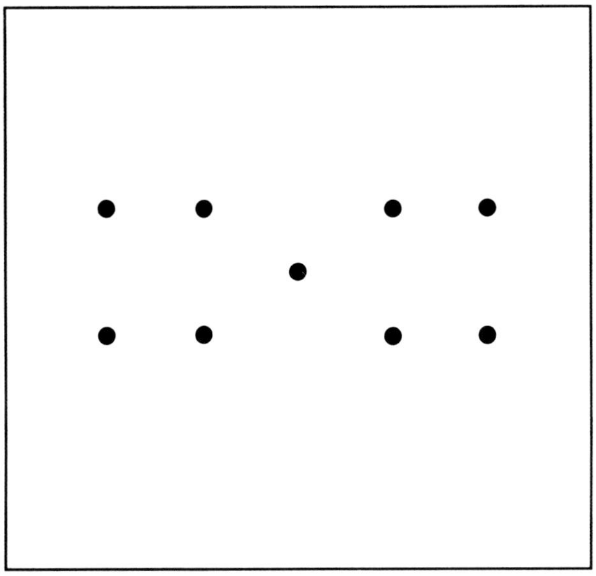

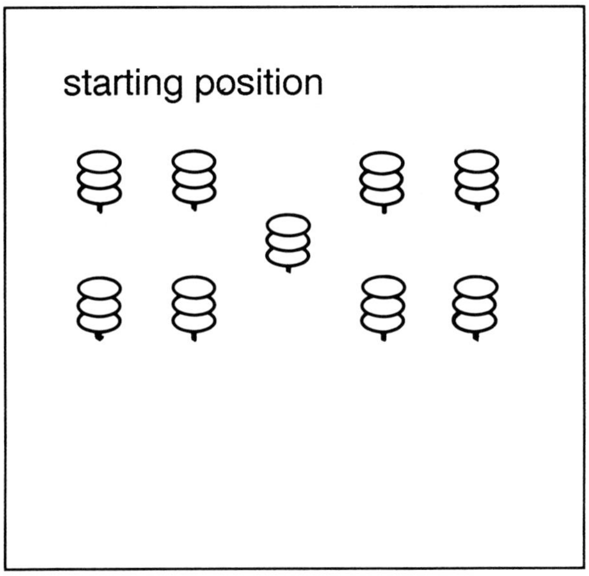

Variation – the player who picks up the last counter is the winner
– pick up more or fewer counters each turn.

BLACK HOLE

Aim

To be the first player to remove all his/her counters from the gameboard.

Number of players

2

Materials

Gameboard (Worksheet 35), ten counters for each player (different colours).

Play

Starter: arrange counters on gameboard (see 'starting position').

- Players take turns to move a counter by:
  - transferring the counter to any empty place next to its original position along a line **or**
  - jumping over one of his or her own counters and removing the jumped counter. More than one jump is permitted.
- Game continues until players have one counter left. This may be removed by moving it into the black hole in the middle. (Note – only the final counter may be removed by placement in the black hole.)

Gameboard

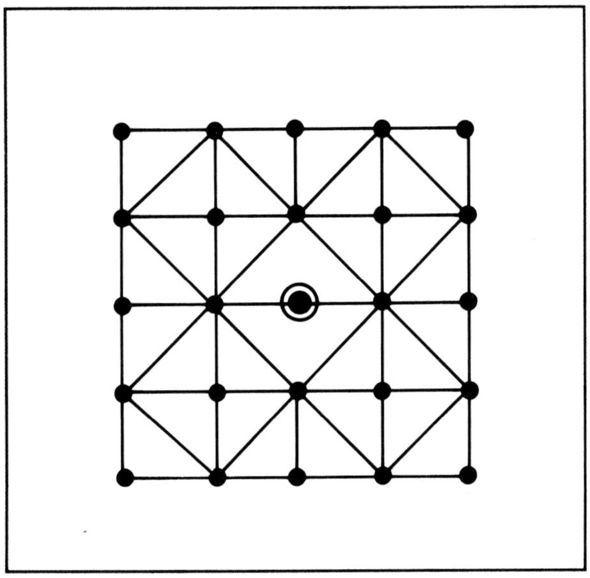

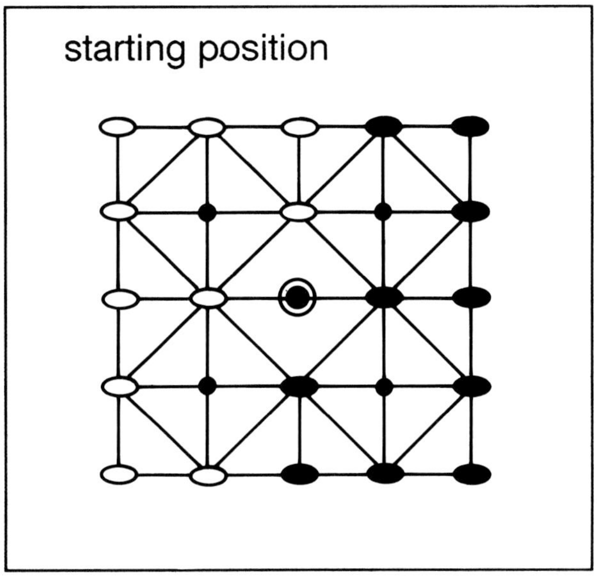

starting position

GAMEBOARD

(Black hole)

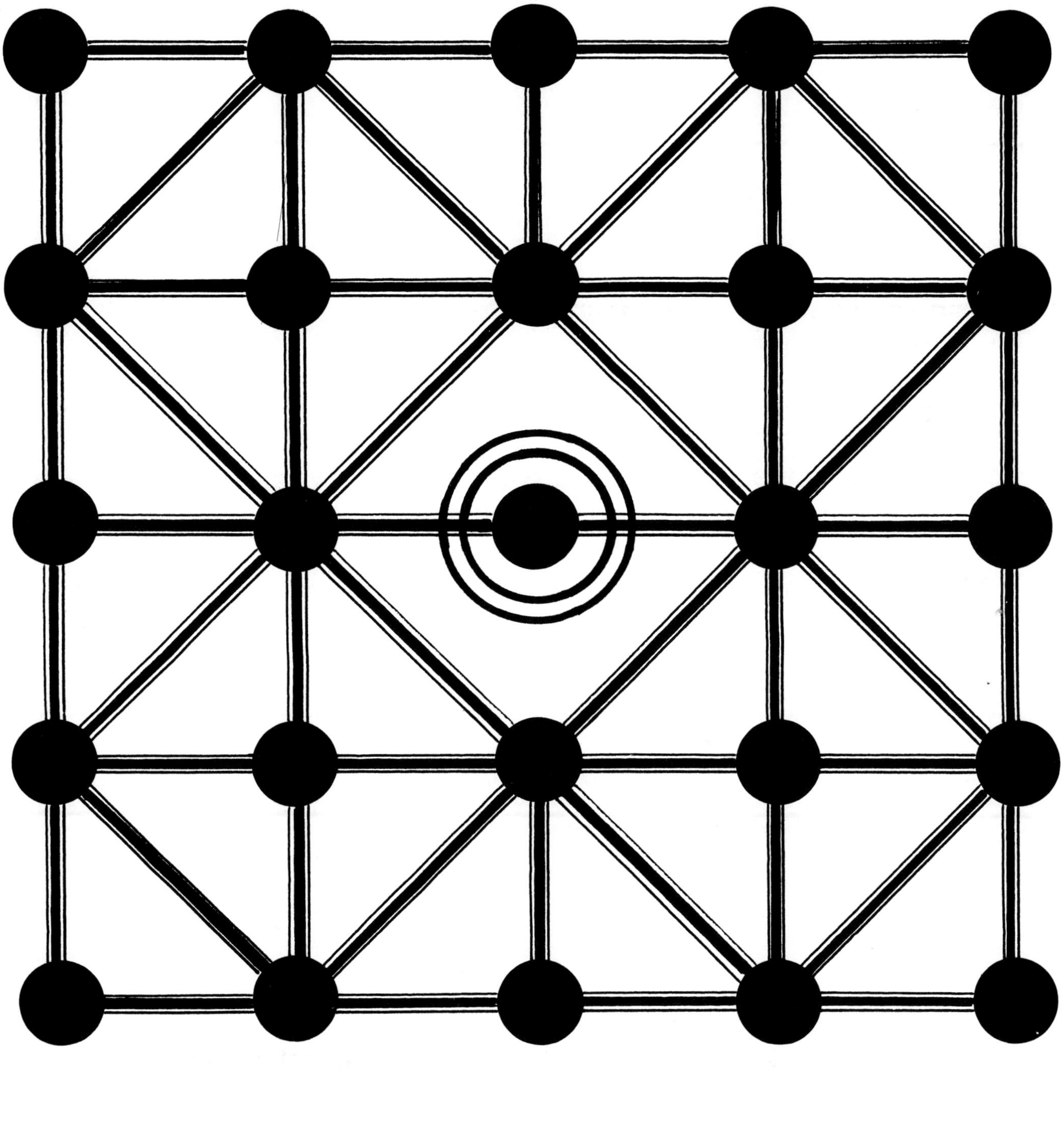

36

STAR GAME

Aim

To claim all of the opponent's counters.

Number of players

2

Materials

Three counters for each player (different colours), paper.

Play

Starter: draw the simple gameboard on the paper (see 'Gameboard') arrange counters (see 'starting position').

- Players take turns to move a counter by jumping on top of an opponent's counter if there is one on the next dot. The player can then claim the counter they jumped on. In any one turn, a player can jump on more than one of his or her opponent's counters if they are all next to each other. If a player is not able to jump on an opponent's counter, he or she must move one of his or her counters to a vacant position next to where it was before.
- Game continues until one of the players has taken all of the opponent's counters.

  This player is the winner. (A draw occurs when neither player can win.)

Gameboard

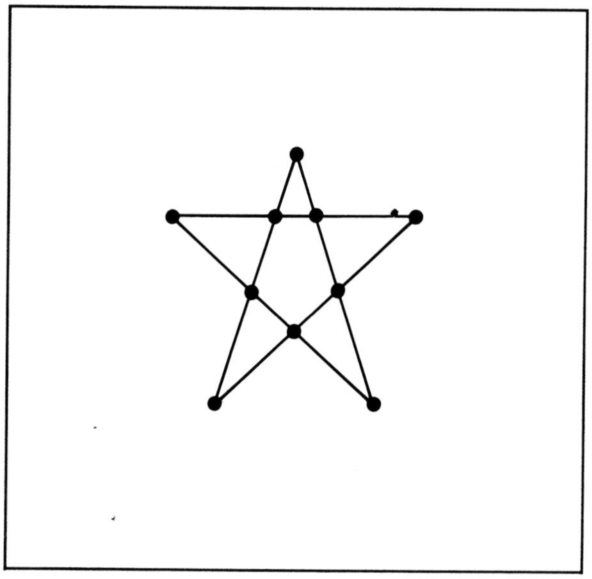

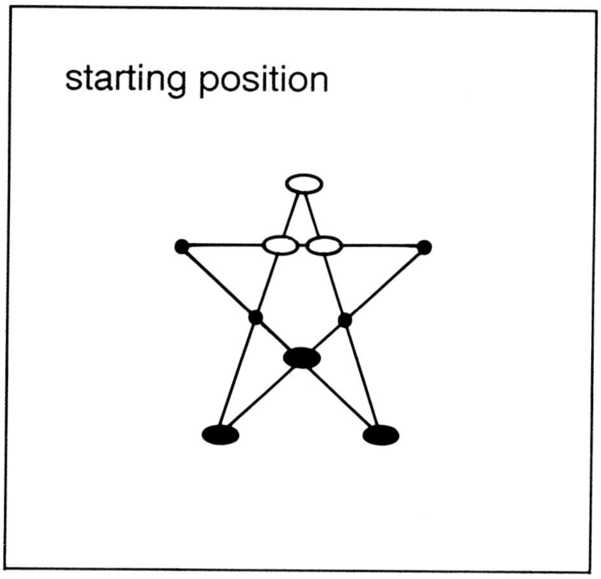

37 REMOVAL

Aim

To find the smallest number of moves necessary to remove all but one of the counters from the gameboard.

Number of players

1

Materials

Gameboard (Worksheets 38 and 39), twelve counters.

Play

Starter: place counters on dots marked 'o' on the gameboard.

- Player moves counters, one at a time, by jumping a single counter to the next vacant dot along a line. The jumped counter is removed.
- Play continues until all but one of the counters have been removed.
- The player keeps a note of his or her moves on a spare copy of the gameboard.

Extension:

- How many different 'ending positions' can you find?
- Can you complete the game leaving the final counter on a chosen dot, e.g. the central dot?

GAMEBOARD

38

(Removal)

B

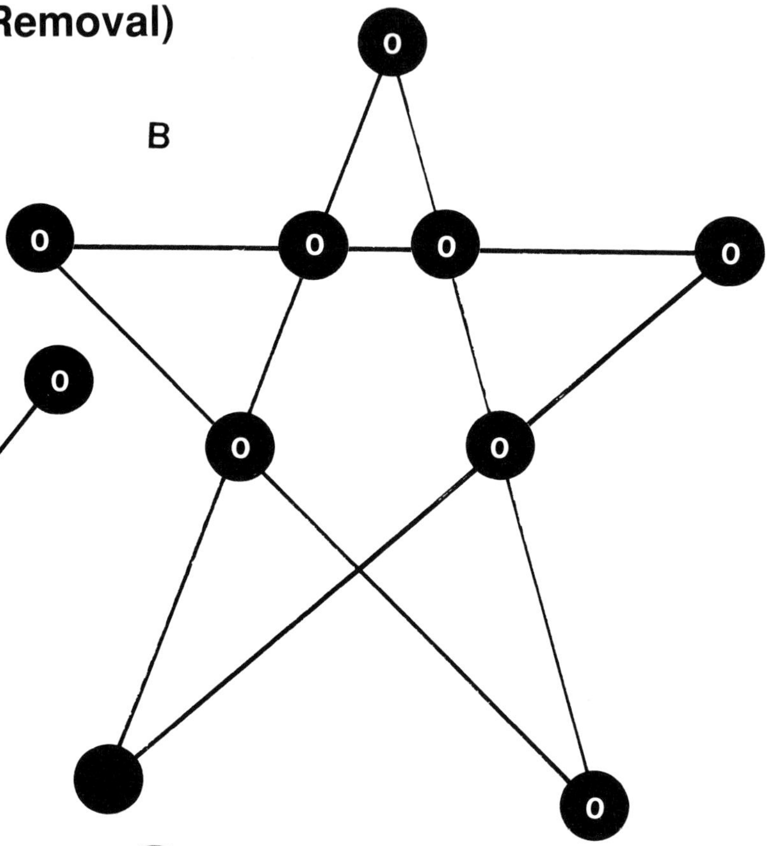

A

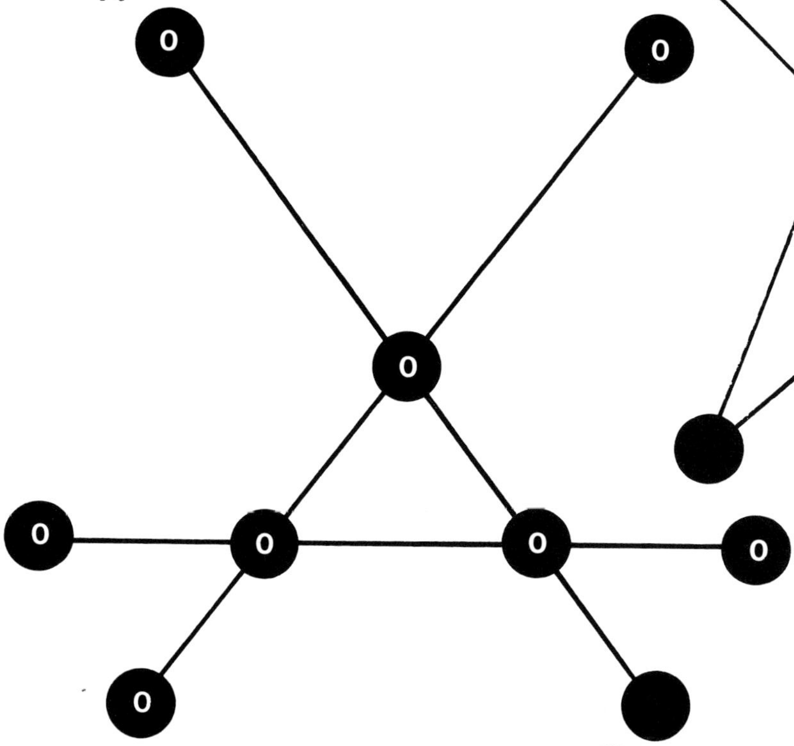

C

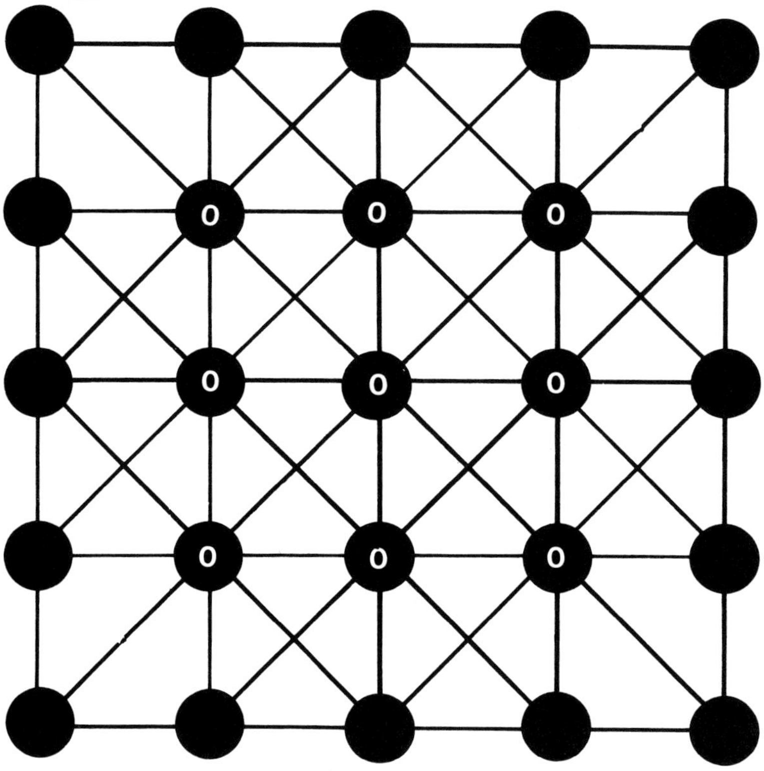

GAMEBOARD

(Removal)

D

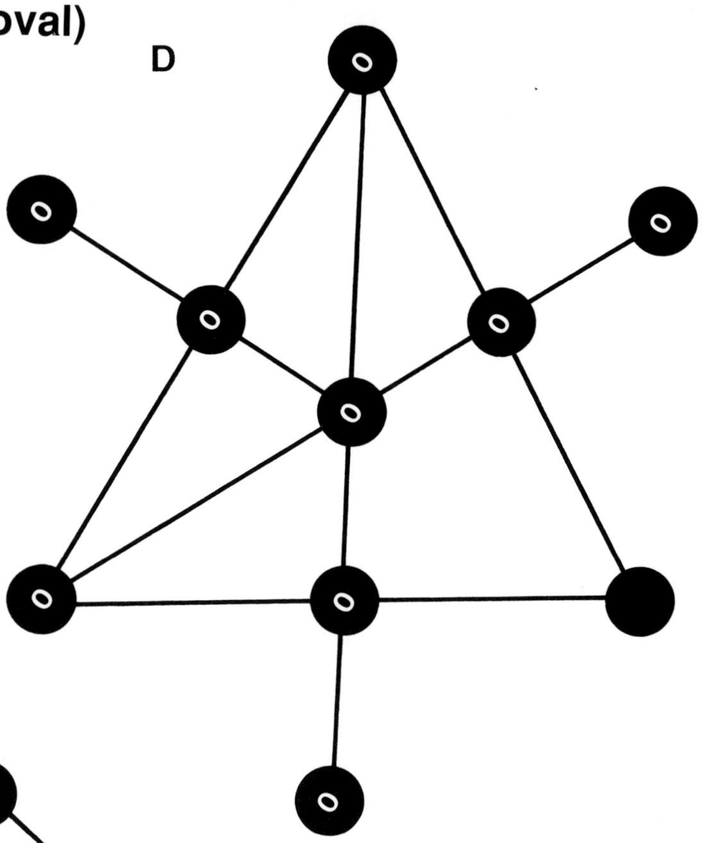

E

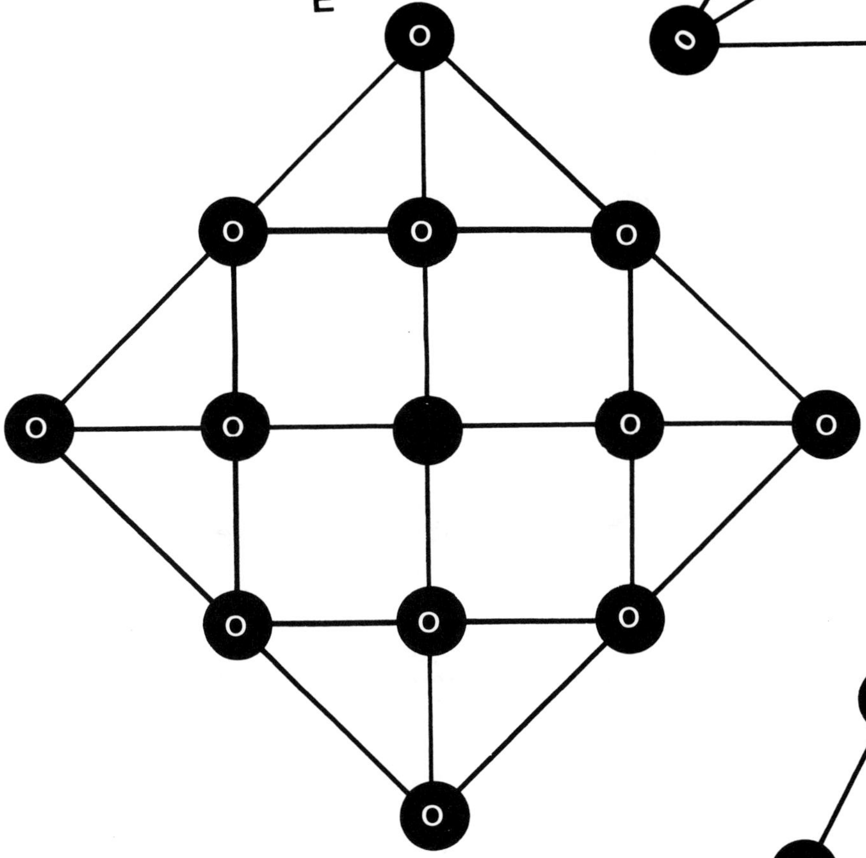

F

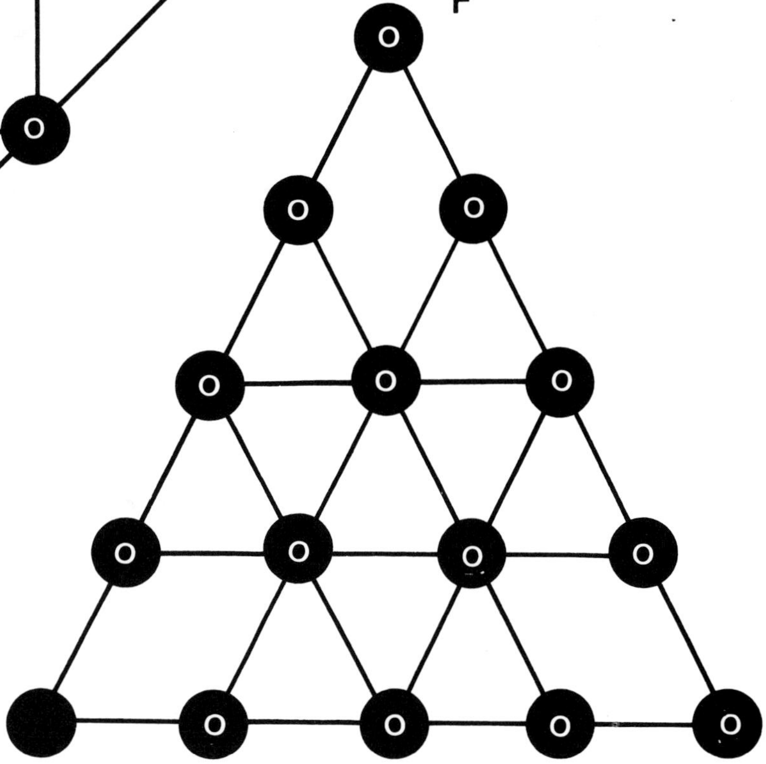

Teacher's checklist

Names	Can understand instructions/follow rules	Can explain instructions clearly to others	Can work out a strategy for a succesful outcome	Can express a preference for a game and give reasons	Able to concentrate (continues until the activity is completed)	Able to take turns and play fairly	Copes with defeat!	**Advanced** Able to record or explain how the problem was resolved	Able to discuss winning strategies	Extends the activity or game

Pupil's own checklist

Name .... Date ....

Games I have played	Children who played with me	Games I have won	Games I liked	Comment

The activities in this book support the following requirements in the National Curriculum Programmes of Study and the Scottish 5-14 Curriculum Guidelines.

National Curriculum: Mathematics

AT1 *Pupils should:*
- be given opportunities to use and apply mathematics in practical tasks, in real-life problems and within mathematics itself;
- be given opportunities to explain their thinking to support the development of their reasoning;
- be taught to develop different mathematical approaches and look for ways to overcome difficulties;
- discuss their work, responding to and asking mathematical questions;
- be taught to recognise simple patterns and relationships and make related predictions about them;
- ask questions including 'What would happen if?' and 'Why?'.

AT2 *Pupils should:*
- develop flexible methods of working with number, orally and mentally;
- use a variety of practical resources and contexts.

National Curriculum: English

AT1 *Pupils should:*
- be given opportunities to talk for a range of purposes;
- be encouraged to listen with growing concentration, and to ask and answer questions that clarify their understanding;
- use talk to develop their thinking.

Scottish 5-14 Guidelines: Mathematics

Problem-solving and Enquiry *Pupils should:*
- in problem-solving activities, be challenged to think about what they are doing, to question and explain;
- consider what factors might be relevant;
- decide how to proceed;
- implement strategies, reasoning logically;
- come to conclusions, recognising patterns, sequences and simple relationships;
- report on a task for a range of purposes and audiences.

Scottish 5-14 Guidelines: English Language

Listening *Pupils should:*
- listen to texts which contain items of information, instructions or directions and show that they understand and can use what has been heard.

Talking *Pupils should:*
- talk to convey items of information, instruction or directions;
- talk to others in a group and contribute appropriately to the purpose of the activity.